THE BUSINESS OF WELLNESS

An Entrepreneur's Guide to Growth and Purpose

by

SEBASTIAN HILBERT

Cover design by Veronica Coello
Interior design by Amit Dey

Published by:
Something or Other Publishing LLC
Brooklyn, Wisconsin 53521
For general inquiries: Info@SOOPLLC.com
For bulk orders: Orders@SOOPLLC.com

Printed in the United States of America
First Printing: 2023

ISBN: 978-1-954102-04-0
Library of Congress Control Number: 2023937516

CONTENTS

Find your inspiration to speak from the heart, tackle your fears, and embark on a venture toward success and meaningful change.

Dedicated to my grandfather and guardian angel,
Manfred Beier, who never had the opportunities I've had.

FOREWORD

IN A CONSTANTLY CHANGING WORLD, we are being challenged more than ever to know our purpose, to live our passions, and to align with the person that we were born to be.

I've been passionate about human potential for more than twenty years. As a high-performance coach and wellness entrepreneur, I've loved seeing people stepping forward and into their own power to truly make a difference in the world. Showing up as the complete and authentic version of ourselves can often initially be frightening. However, to bare all to the world is one of the greatest gifts we can offer humanity – for the journey that we must embark on to reach our own summit often provides the most powerful lessons of them all.

One of my favorite quotes by the highly acclaimed American Football Coach, Vince Lombardi, was this: "The will to win is not nearly as important as the will to prepare to win." It has rung true for my personal and professional wellness journey to now.

Holistic preparation allows us to be ready – mentally, physically, and spiritually – to face the boulders that often show up in life and business as we navigate down our own entrepreneurial stream. These boulders often appear on a daily basis in the form of unique micro-moments. These moments allow us to face hard truths, to become more flexible in our thinking, but most importantly, to learn how to adapt more quickly and effectively. After all, the speed of adaptation is our greatest tool in the current age.

The Business of Wellness: An Entrepreneur's Guide to Growth and Purpose is perhaps one of the most important reads for anyone who is seeking the best ways to prepare to win in their own modern-day wellness story. Sebastian Hilbert is a master of authenticity and adaptation; the information that he has laid out in this book provides you with the ultimate entrepreneurial roadmap. Moreover, it imparts wisdom from Sebastian's own purpose, passion, and alignment for a subject that is changing the game when it comes to how we approach and master the art of genuine wellness.

In this book, Sebastian provides us with valuable insight into the Inner Game – understanding that to be able to give to others, we must be willing to give to ourselves first; and for us to help enhance the world, we must also be willing to evolve.

From all the amazing lessons that you will find in this book, perhaps the most important piece to remember is that success is not linear but rather multi-dimensional. This book is your manual, your coach, and your mentor toward helping you create a successful wellness business and, more so, a successful life in itself.

James Yates
High-performance coach, wellness entrepreneur,
and the founder of Reignite Enterprises

HOW TO USE THIS BOOK

I HAVE WRITTEN THIS book so you can read it front to back and feel entertained by the stories and hopefully experience a mind shift of your own. It's a pathway for you to learn about how to build a thriving wellness business and become an impactful wellness entrepreneur.

Furthermore, should you at any stage be seeking advice in your business or personal growth, this book can be used to quickly find chapters most relevant to your position. The knowledge therein can serve to guide your next steps.

Growth in business is a process that occurs on the inside through personal growth and on the outside through strategies and systems. This is the reason why the book is divided into two parts, your "Inner Game" and your "Outer Game". Most challenges you will have to face are a combination of both. Thus, before selecting the right chapter, you must first understand what's underneath the problem you are facing. To make this easier, refer back to the Inner Game as you read the chapters in the Outer Game, by referencing Inner Game principles which you can then easily look up in the first part of the book. Living true to your values and purpose is a constant back and forth between your inner growth and your outer actions. Both are intrinsically linked.

Reading through the book front to back will give you a deep understanding of how your purpose and underlying values feed into what you do in your business so that you are always in alignment with who you truly are and what you stand for.

There are a couple of basic concepts I recommend you read first so you understand where everything else you will read comes from. You can find this at the beginning of this book before the Inner Game chapters begin, but once you understand the basics you can read any chapter separately to extract the information you need right now.

I know we all get busy with life. When you are in business for yourself, it is especially tough to make time to learn more about how to work on your business rather than in your business. This is the reason why it is really vital to me that you get the right advice anytime you need it.

PART I

An Introduction
to Wellness

1

THE INFLUENCER ECONOMY

"Change is the only constant in life."

—Heraclitus

IN TODAY'S WORLD, AND especially among younger generations, people are increasingly moving away from mass media, preferring to follow influencers for advice and information. Anyone can be an influencer: celebrities, entrepreneurs, and any other type of content creator on channels like YouTube and social media.

People on this trend might watch daily videos from Leonardo DiCaprio about environmental change or follow Michael Gregers for nutritional advice. "Doctor Mike" has seven million YouTube subscribers. These influencers have great power when it comes to recommending products and services, which opens up great opportunities but also great danger.

Distribution on social media, websites, forums, and so forth has created the possibility to reach a great number of people. Because it's a person rather than general news or an anonymous documentary that is passing on information, influencers are much more personal and authentic. Real people sharing with real people builds powerful connections.

I see you sitting there reading this book and I know what you're thinking: that's nice and all but the problem is that there is no regulation about what these influencers share. Anyone can share anything without qualification.

Which brings us to the danger I was talking about. Anyone can influence anyone for the better or worse. You can say that it is for the worse and ignore the opportunity, sitting like a bulwark against the future. However, many of these influencers are sharing scientifically proven information. Are they always correct? Probably not, but the information is funneled through a clearer channel than newspapers, TV, and magazines. Since influencers are not anonymous, they can be engaged in discussion and challenged by their audience.

In the small German village where I grew up, the downfall of one-way media is clearly sign-posted. There, the older generation obstructs the path of the young, shutting down new thoughts and behaviors. But these novelties are undeniable and must be dealt with.

You cannot stop progress.

All you can do is learn about where the world is heading and take action to push progress in the right direction. As students and professionals in the fields of health, wellness, and lifestyle, I am certain most readers are *au fait* with Yin and Yang, the duality of things, and the fact that everything has a good and a bad side.

This new Influencer Economy can be your springboard to the lifestyle business of your dreams, enabling you to finally make the impact you desire, or it can keep you in your corner, watching everyone else fly past as you grow steadily more frustrated.

Think back fifty or a hundred years ago. If you wanted to make an impact and reach a large number of people with your business, you had to have a lot of money. Back then, only the wealthy could build a factory, rent offices, and pay for mass media advertising. The barriers for entry to any kind of business were enormous.

All that most people could do was get a job, do what they were told, and bury their dreams. Well, that's what it was like in East Germany where I grew up anyway, but little has changed since then. Our children are educated in a system that does not support problem-solving skills, free thinking, or basic life skills around money, relationships, and health.

That said, change is coming and especially the younger generation is waking up and demanding more than a "secure job and pension." Now you can reach anyone at any time for free. You can start and run your own business with your mobile phone in the back of a taxi (sorry, I should say Uber). The world is literally at your fingertips all the time.

The Wellness Industry in particular is one of the fastest growing industries with a combined annual revenue of US$4.2 trillion, that's 4.2 million million dollars, and an average growth of 12 percent. In essence, it is exploding.

You will find a lot of people online who share great information regularly, building and educating their audiences. One of my favorites is Dr. Greger with his nutritionfacts.org on YouTube and his website which has over 500,000 subscribers and millions of views on his short fact- and science-based videos. Best of all, he does not allow advertising. He wants to stay independent and not be driven by profit.

Does he make a decent living and impact the world? You bet! There are ways to make this work without turning to the dark side. There are thousands of people out there sharing their truth and creating change in an authentic and genuine manner.

You too can create your lifestyle business and have the impact you desire. To do this the right way, it's crucial to tap deeply into who you truly are and what you stand for, so you can define clear guidelines and an authentic direction that is more than about making money.

2

WHY I WROTE THIS BOOK

"Whatever be the nature of business, fundamentally it has all been started in the interest of the wellbeing of human beings. The business of human wellbeing is the only real business. All other businesses are subsidiaries of that."

—Sadhguru,
Yogi and Founder of the Isha Foundation

DESPITE THE MASSIVE GROWTH in the Wellness Industry, there is a sustained attack on the alternative health industry because it doesn't "fit the model" of the lucrative pharmaceutical and medical industry. It's like 'the rails are broken at the top of a cliff' and instead of focusing on fixing the rails, we continue to build faster ambulances at the bottom.'

I am not saying there is no place for ambulances, hospitals, and pharmaceuticals. What I am saying is that the focus is wrong and we are not incentivizing the transition to wellness and preventative behavior through government actions.

In 2019, 16 natural therapies were excluded from private health insurance rebates in Australia.[1] What kind of message does that send? It's the wrong direction. It's not focusing on fixing the rails.

I mean how can it be that nutritional education is optional when studying to become a general practitioner, nurse, or other medical professional? That's the case all over the world. And then people go to their general practitioner asking for advice about their diet. This contradiction seems complete madness to me.

How many health professionals and people in general actually know about lifestyle medicine and nutrition? There is a massive disproportion of people who have close to no education about nutrition and how the body works, let alone the complex interplay of energies innate to all humans.

The internet is full of information, but as discussed previously, anyone can publish their views. The result: we have the good and the bad.

Most importantly, it's incredibly difficult to know what is and isn't true. This is especially true for subjects where there are massive lobbies working against information that is beneficial to people. If you read two opposing articles on a topic, how do you know which one is true? Both may use substantiated facts and demonstrate a clear case for their argument. But how do you know if it's the whole truth? How do you know that the writer has not cherry-picked information to support his point of view?

---

[1] "Natural Therapies Review," NHMRC, accessed 20 April 2023, https://www.nhmrc.gov.au/health-advice/all-topics/complementary-medicines/natural-therapies-review.

3

OUR BROKEN HEALTH SYSTEM

"The doctor of the future will give no medicine but will interest his patients in the care of the human frame, in diet and in the cause and prevention of disease."

—Thomas Edison

PEOPLE WHO ARE SEARCHING for better health with the use of fewer pharmaceuticals face vast and contradictory information online, when it comes to holistic health and well-being. In some cases, practitioners and healers don't have a scientific explanation for why their modalities and treatments work. We just know they do. Look at spiritual healing, for instance, or energy-related treatments.

However, there is one big advantage! Alternative treatments, wellness coaching, lifestyle medicine, whole-food plant-based diets, spiritual healing, channeling, and so on, can all be beneficial to some extent. There are numerous cases where we can show incredible results and life-changing experiences from such alternative forms of self-care. The results are there and that is the reason why this industry is growing rapidly. Despite many governments' publishing policies that work against the wellness industry and propagate misinformation (on both sides), this area of health and well-being is growing strongly because there is nothing anyone can do about people telling people how amazing they feel and how many lives have been saved through these forms of self-care. That is the true power, and eventually science will follow.

As a holistic practitioner or wellness professional, you need to stay strong and be persistent with your message so that the world keeps going in the right direction. This is what has driven me to help you. It's what I want to bring into this world. I want you to keep going and not only "hang in there" but thrive and spread your message as far as possible to create more stories, get more people talking, and eventually to change the governments', and all peoples', minds for the better, moving the world to sustainable wellness.

Many of my family and friends suffer from preventable diseases like diabetes, cardiovascular disease, and cancer. My grandfather died of cancer, my grandmother has type 2 diabetes, and my mother is hypertensive, just to name a few.

When I came to Australia in 2010, I learned from alternative health practitioners that many of these diseases are lifestyle-related and pre-ventable. Western medicine is in many ways at its limits, and I want to spread the solution so that others won't have to see their families suffer as much as I have. Now I have made it my mission to empower thera-pists and all wellness business owners to reach out and help more people so that the world moves toward better health and well-being.

4

SUSTAINABLE WELLNESS

"There are a thousand hacking at the branches of evil to one who is striking at the root..."

—Henry David Thoreau, Walden

MY VISION IS TO MOVE the world to sustainable wellness.

There are two parts to this: Sustainability and Wellness. We already talked about Wellness, the second part of my vision, and many readers will know much about this already.

Sustainability, on the other hand, might not be your wheelhouse. So, before we move on, let me explain.

Sustainability in the environmental sense means "the quality of not being harmful to the environment or depleting natural resources, and thereby supporting long-term ecological balance."[2]

My goal is to combine sustainability with wellness, thereby moving the world to wellness, protecting the environment, and supporting a long-term ecological balance. Wellness needs to be in balance with the planet.

---

[2] Sustainability Definition & Meaning | Dictionary.com

It is not just about being healthy and well, but also about being environmentally conscious so we not only sustain ourselves but everyone and everything else as well. The environment has always been a big driver for me, influencing me since before I even moved to Australia and discovered alternative treatments and lifestyle medicine.

I am always careful to listen for new ways to live. I took short showers, drove my car consciously to use less fuel, and started recycling. These are all good things, but as Australia helped me make new discoveries around health, it was there that I also made a disturbing discovery about the environment.

If we look at current efforts to stop the depletion of the earth's resources and prevent greenhouse gasses, we are pitifully far from achieving our goals. Many people think the solutions to climate change lie in electric cars, battery-powered homes, and factories fueled by renewable energy sources like solar, hydro, and wind. These technologies are phenomenal and I am a big supporter of them. However, thinking that we can solve the issue with our current technology is simply delusional.

What NASA scientist James Hansen wrote in 2011 holds true despite what some politicians propose: "Suggesting that renewables will let us phase rapidly off fossil fuels in the United States, China, India or the world as a whole is almost the equivalent of believing in the Easter bunny and tooth fairy."[3] At the time, this message angered me. How can someone be so pessimistic and not believe in humanity?

In an article I read in mid-2019 in *The Australian*,[4] the current situation and misconceptions are described as thus:

The promises made in Rio de Janeiro in 1992 and the Kyoto Treaty in 1997 fell apart. A new study of the promises made under the Paris Agreement of 2015 finds that of almost 200 signatories, only 17

---

[3] Matthew Nisbet, "The McKibben Doctrine: How Deep Green Politics Undermine Climate Action," May 20, 2013, https://thebreakthrough.org/articles/the-mckibben-doctrine.

[4] Bjorn Lomburg, "The Great Climate Myth," *The Weekend Australian*, June 15-16, 2019, https://drive.google.com/file/d/18DhtfFgo14JP3kom6BgE2WDzKEXvPWYy/view?usp=sharing.

countries – the likes of Samoa and Algeria – are living up to them, and these are succeeding mostly because they promised so little. But even if every country did everything promised in the Paris Agreement, the emission cuts by 2030 would add up to only one percent of what would be needed to keep temperature rises to under two degrees Celsius.

The reason for this miniscule impact is due mostly to the inefficiency and unreliability of renewable energy resources. We may see more solar farms and solar panels on roofs and more wind farms put up, but the world's energy use is also growing rapidly. All energy resources are following this trend, but there is no shift in balance to renewables or in fact to any other resource. We are simply expanding in all areas.

Higher energy consumption is directly proportional to higher living standards, better health, and longer life expectancy. How much energy do we need to bring preventative health and well-being to the world? How much water, electricity, and other limited resources? Don't get me wrong: As I said, I support technology and especially bringing wellness to every part of the planet, but progress needs to be sustainable. Most practitioners are well aware of the environmental issues but more often than not we are not looking at the actual numbers. We get really passionate about plastic straws in the ocean but are unaware that they make up only 0.03 percent of all plastic in the ocean. How many people know that the real culprits are the fishing nets that make up almost 50 percent?[5]

These kinds of misconceptions about the environment are very common. As within the health system and the distribution of false information, there is a huge imbalance in the information that needs to be spread. This is due to the hyped-up information that we see all the time. What would you do if something was out of balance and you knew it was caused by different factors? Let's say you look at a traditional scale that has too much weight on one side compared to the other

[5] " Evidence that the Great Pacific Garbage Patch is rapidly accumulating plastic," published 22 March 2018, https://www.nature.com/articles/s41598-018-22939-w.

and there are different weights on it. A few heavy weights and several small weights are tipping the scale all the way to the max on one side. How would you bring the scale back into balance?

Would you focus on the small weights like plastic straws, although you can clearly see that they make almost no difference? Even if you removed all of them, it would barely affect the balance. Or would you focus on taking off one big weight that makes an enormous difference, providing a real shift toward solving the problem?

Without taking this any further into health and social justice, my intention is to show you what makes the biggest negative impact on our environment and what sustainable wellness means to me. Sustainability goes even beyond the environment for me and brings in spiritual and personal growth. It's an individual journey within all of us. I am not asking anything of you here, but I know the environment is something that is close to all our hearts. Sharing this kind of information has made me realize a few significant things in life, one of the most important being that we can shift the scale of environmental sustainability quickly by adopting a plant-based diet.

This is not a book about animal justice. We all have our own journey; nobody can be forced to change and the negative judgment of others does not help in any case.

Now, let's clear our minds, take a deep breath, and find our way back to focusing on your wellness business journey.

PART II

The Inner Game

UNDERSTANDING THE INNER GAME

"The size of your business is a direct reflection of your inner growth and therefore the crucial factor in your capacity to change the world."

—Sebastian Hilbert

LET ME TELL YOU A little story that I heard a few years ago. There was a priest in his early twenties who, with all his courage, energy, and enthusiasm, wanted to change the world. He strived to make the world a better place but soon realized, in his thirties, that this was beyond his power.

So, the priest decided to focus on his local community and only change them. Soon after, he realized again that this was beyond his power. He contemplated disappointedly and then, in his forties, decided to spend more time with his family and friends to change them for the better. Over the next years, he tried to change his family and friends, showing them how they could live a better life. Again, he was unsuccessful and soon fell terribly ill. Before his death, he reflected:

"If I had only changed myself, I may have changed my family and – who knows – perhaps even the world."

This rather sad story always reminds me of the biggest lesson I have learned so far in my short life. You can't force change on anyone in the world. All you can do is to focus on changing yourself. Become an awakened, more conscious person, and with that you will have the ability to flow through life and impact as many people as you want. But you need to let people choose for themselves and not worry about those who are not ready.

Everyone has their own journey and does the best they can.

We need to stop worrying about judgment and rejection and leave our perfectionism behind to truly evolve and move the world toward our vision.

The next pages will be about my learnings and experiences of self-development and inner growth so you may learn new things and be reminded of some important universal lessons.

Some things we need to hear many times and different ways to let them truly sink in and make a change.

1

LIFE'S WHISPERS

"Don't let the noise of others' opinions drown out your own inner voice. And most importantly, have the courage to follow your heart and intuition. They somehow already know what you truly want to become. Everything else is secondary."

—Steve Jobs

IN THE YEAR THAT I wrote this book, I was building my own digital marketing business after finishing my studies with honors and Dux at one of the world's most prestigious hotel management schools. Up to that point, almost everything in my life was strongly influenced by others and I didn't know how to tap into what I truly wanted. How do you ask yourself the right questions? How do you honestly facilitate this inner exploration if nobody ever taught you how? And most importantly, how do you make space in your life for this, when everyone around you already seems to tell you what's best?

Society sets you up to become a cog in a machine, to earn and consume, to buy a house and have a family, to work, not to complain and to be yourself. I felt lost and I didn't approve, so I changed my path. I believe that at any point in your life, the universe, God, Gaia, or whatever you want to call it, very gently nudges you into the "right" direction. All you have to do is feel into it and recognize the signs. However, if you ignore these whispers, they will turn into a knockout blow, like a hammer to the head.

This happened to me in 2008, in Germany, when I was three years into my first attempt at a degree. I was pretending to study a subject that I had chosen because everyone told me it would be great for me. The hammer blow came during that year because I had ignored the signs. I confessed to my parents I was taking drugs, my grandfather whom I loved so dearly had died, and I was in a car crash, which almost killed my best friend and me. I was crushed. A mighty hammer from above, indeed.

I remember walking to the hospital park, dragging my plastic bag mounted on a metal trolley with a tube coming out of my chest to drain the fluid around my collapsed lung. The only people who would go out there were smokers and everyone else in the hospital looked at me disapprovingly when I passed – clearly assuming I was going for a smoke with a severe issue with my lungs. The walk of shame. But I didn't care; I needed to think and the hospital room wasn't the right place. In that park, in the summer of 2008, I made a decision. I decided to change my life completely. The hammer had been felt.

In hindsight, I realize that this experience created space for me to pause, reflect, and make a decision from the inside out – not for others, not to conform, not for what was expected of me, but simply from a place that felt raw and completely me. It took a lot of pain and strife for me to get there.

Creating space is a game-changer and what happened to me in 2008 happened all over again with the global COVID-19 pandemic of 2020. Even if you are reading this book and this pandemic is long over, I am certain it has not been completely forgotten. On one hand, it was a big hammer for humanity, for we as a collective had been ignoring the signs too. On the other hand, all of a sudden, many people had more time than they had ever had before. Less work, less stress, and the opportunity to spend time with the activities, hobbies, and the people that really matter (or those that don't). Covid has given us the space to reflect and realize that something is wrong.

I want to acknowledge that there are people who now need to work more, who have less time and more stress like our health workers around the world. COVID-19 has created a lot of suffering and, with many of my friends and my whole family being in Europe, I am well aware of the death, isolation, and fear the pandemic has created. However, a big blow with a hammer undoubtedly comes with pain. The important factor is that we learn and come out the other side with a new understanding and better ways to live. We need to learn how to pause and create space for OURSELVES so that we can make decisions that we can truly stand behind and start living a purposeful life of joy and balance.

When Covid hit in early 2020, I had caught myself just before a serious burnout. Losing 80 percent of our business revenue forced me to pause, like so many others. My goal of becoming a digital marketer and global influencer bound me to my computer, phone, and iPad for up to eighty hours a week, and, thanks to my German nature, I went through every wall headfirst. Did it work? You bet! Did it feel congruent and aligned with who I wanted to be? Certainly not! My relationship with my partner was on the edge every day and I felt so exhausted that I couldn't even make a decent meal or have a light chat with my partner. Everything was a fight!

I decided to stop and spend three months reflecting on my vision and purpose. Now I have a clear vision and non-negotiable values to live by. The moment I started making decisions purely from those values in alignment with that vision, everything fell into place. I rediscovered what I love doing, who I truly want to be, and how I want to contribute to this world.

A 2021 study by the Global Wellness Institute states: "The global wellness economy stands at $4.4 trillion in 2020 amidst the chaos and disruptions caused by COVID-19." It fell by 11 percent from 2020 but is expected to grow to nearly $7 trillion by 2025. Wellness tourism alone is at $435 billion and although it declined rapidly as a result of the pandemic, wellness tourism decreased less than overall tourism.[6] Looking at the world after Covid, it seems that more and more people are trying to escape their lives but then come back to do the same things over and over again, ignoring the whispers, enduring the big blows, and hoping that something changes. The world is in desperate need of a different way of life. We need to create spaces where people can completely disconnect from their stressful lives and receive the guidance to ask the right questions. A place to strip away the facade, rejuvenate the mind, body, and soul so that we can create something new to unite that which we truly are – individually and as a whole.

It was then that the idea came to me to fulfill my vision of moving the world to sustainable wellness. With this in mind, I decided to build a network of sanctuaries worldwide that provide unique spaces in nature and a process to make true life-changing experiences as easy and sustainable as possible.

These sanctuaries are unlike any other standard hotel spa, luxury retreat, and wellness escape. It provides not only a completely flexible and environmentally friendly space but also a process that ensures true transformation for anyone to create a life of purpose and true joy. Sustainability goes beyond the environment and into people's everyday lives on many levels. The need for wellness and well-being is growing fast and the world is clearly telling us to do something.

This goal was the fallout of COVID-19 for me, but not only in the sense that it created clear values and a different way of life. I started to make big changes in my business and somehow everything started

---

[6] *The Global Wellness Economy: Looking Beyond COVID*, Global Wellness Institute, December 2021, https://globalwellnessinstitute.org/industry-research/the-global-wellness-economy-looking-beyond-covid/.

working out. It was as if the universe had finally given way and said, "You got it, let's go!"

The biggest challenge at that point was for me to trust the process. The goal of creating a network of wellness sanctuaries around the world felt like having to climb Mount Everest twice in a row with no experience or the requisite resources. However, when I shared my vision of that place of purpose and joy, I always found the next step on my path. That's all you need to progress, isn't it? As long as you have the next step, the journey is pretty straight forward, isn't it? This raises the real question, though: Will you have the courage to trust that you will find that next step of many toward a goal you can't even imagine?

Courage was the real challenge for me, but to reach that understanding took a long time. The starting point is looking for answers about how you can grow your business while staying in alignment with your values. To do this, one must first understand one's flow. Let's make sure we get the first step right: finding your vision, purpose, and what truly matters to you.

2

CREATING SPACE

"The path to our destination is not always a straight one. We go down the wrong road, we get lost, we turn back. Maybe it doesn't matter which road we embark on. Maybe what matters is that we embark."

—Barbara Hall

I REMEMBER WATCHING A TedTalk that outlined the five most important factors for employees to stay loyal to a company and perform well. Guess what was not in the top three. Money! Having ownership of tasks, sections, projects, and so forth, and responsibility for their outcomes were at the top. This survey showed that employees want to feel valued and needed. We all want that, don't we? But at the very top of the list you could see this phrase: "Something bigger than themselves".

They wanted to be part of something big. Something that made them feel as if they were all working together toward a goal that had a positive impact on the world. I really started thinking about this survey and how it applied to my little web design and online marketing business. "Model yourself after the big guys, they are clearly doing something right when it comes to business," one of my early mentors said to me.

So, whenever I see or hear big companies doing something very successfully, I try to apply it to my business. Applying others' successful strategies has worked for me over the years, and I highly recommend that you do the same. There are almost no limitations to this. You can apply anything to your own business by adapting it to suit your purposes.

The hard part is adapting something to suit your business so that it's not only practical and feasible, but also successful. So, I started thinking about this idea of "something bigger than oneself". It was at a very early stage in my business experience when I started Googling about my "Why" (or *raison d'être*, as the French call it), my vision, mission, and values. One of the most inspiring pieces of advice I found was a TedTalk by Simon Sinek called "Start With Why".

After listening to Simon Sinek, I had a job to do. I needed to find my Why and my mission. During this process, I realized that to share my mission with others, I had to define it clearly and concisely. However, even after I defined my vision, I recognized that I didn't truly understand myself. Therefore, I never deeply embraced my vision in a way that brought me joy. This is an absolutely crucial part. Writing a vision that is beautiful and has an impact on the world is not sufficient because that vision needs to align deeply with who you are as a conscious human being. Once you have achieved that alignment by sharing it with others, thereby attracting incredible people into your life and feeling content and grounded, joy will come easily to you.

When I first wrote down my vision – or at least a first version of it – I didn't have that alignment and the confidence to share my vision authentically. I continued to mold my vision, digging from the inside out and created the space in my life to dig deeply and explore who I truly was. Creating the space for yourself to strip away everything that doesn't belong to you emotionally and spiritually so you can rejuvenate your heart, soul, and mind is essential for building oneself anew.

I had always been lacking alignment between my vision and myself. I had a vision but it was a sideshow and not my guiding star. My efforts in business were still about how to make ends meet, not to fulfill my vision. Making ends meet didn't make much of a difference since other problems would arise that added to the struggles. Once I found the values I truly believed in and that expressed who I was, along with the actions and missions that brought me joy, my success in life and business started to come together.

You need something more than money to be in business and become a leader in your field. Money just won't cut it. At least not when you are looking for joy and harmony in your life. The masculine world we live in has made us believe that focusing on short-term financial goals and rushing toward them like a bulldozer is the way to happiness. And where has it gotten us? Humanity is becoming more and more isolated, and the world is in a state of climate change and overwhelming health issues, both mentally and physically.

Instead of constantly getting bounced around by the media and the people around us, we need to look inside ourselves and ask some serious questions. Who are we? What brings us joy? When are we in flow? When are we not and what's in between? These journeys do not offer simple answers – they require a lifetime of study. Although lifelong, this pursuit is a beautiful one. As we travel on this journey of self-discovery, we need to tap into your heart and soul, aligning them with the mind. I believe that progress will bring us more joy and success than any answer could. The answers you will get are profound and, if you have the courage, will change your life completely.

I believe that many people who are obsessed with cleaning the house and keeping things tidy or other mundane activities like that are actually using them to distract themselves from their inner work. Inner work is not an easy journey. It will challenge you and the further you go, the bigger the challenges. So, it's easier to keep doing the familiar and say, "I have to do this or that." In other words, you are procrastinating on the work that moves the needle. What's the point of having done all your emails, cleaned the house, and followed up with all your clients if, at the end of the day, you haven't put any effort into writing your book, calling people with whom you would never otherwise talk, or going to an event you are scared to attend? You may feel a sense of achievement but there was no growth.

My experience, and what I have seen with others, shows clearly that the only way to create the growth you desire in any aspect of your life is to dedicate the space it needs. Most people are constantly on the hamster wheel, eating when they are running to work, working overtime, and sleeping too little. Have times when everything stops, when you have no other choice but to retreat inside because you removed the familiar distractions.

Ultimately you need to create this space for yourself. I started by blocking out half a day each week to work on my business. This allowed me to do whatever I wanted as long as it wasn't anything linear like coaching, administration, emails, social media, and so forth. At first, I used this time for hard strategy, but it soon became time for meditation, journaling and reading. Now I have a full day each week, one to two hours every morning, and three days every quarter, when I create the space to tap into my heart and soul and continue on my journey. It's not a burden. I look forward to it!

When you start on this journey, it's important that you do it strategically. Don't try to escape your world. Have the intention to lift yourself to the next level. This can be a very small shift like becoming aware of behavior that doesn't suit you or a big shift where you realize you need to change paths completely. What you get will depend on your readiness for the next step. One part of this journey should always be working on and checking in with your vision. In this way, what is bigger than you will be ingrained. It will be the anchor for your journey, a bit like wakeboarding. You stand on your board holding on to a line attached to the boat. This line pulls you in one direction but you can bounce left and right, jumping over challenging waves, trying out new moves. The further you progress, the better you get. However, the fun part is the process, not the destination.

While your vision remains the same, your mission can change as often as necessary. I started by morphing my business toward holistic practitioners and wellness professionals, which built the foundation for this book. My goal with this book is to help 100,000 practitioners so that they can, in turn, help more people. By achieving that goal, I would be taking one big step toward my vision. During the course of writing this book and checking in with myself, I also have been experiencing the significant shift in my life that I mentioned in the previous chapter, my new alignment. I have a new mission but because it is aligned with the overall vision of everything that I have done, the new mission sits right with me. As I progress on this journey toward inner joy and success, it's as if I'm pulling all the strings of my life together.

This is the journey you need to take. Allow yourself to explore your inner self. Once you get something, use it. It is imperative that you apply it. There will be a constant back-and-forth between your inner development and outer actions. Check in with yourself, take action, repeat. This way you will grow as a person and strengthen who you are. You will build more and more capacity to deal with challenges, adversities, and roadblocks ahead. I wrote this book to help you make a bigger impact in the world, share your message, and help more people. The only way you can do this is to solve big problems which come with big challenges. The person you need to be is the one who can face these challenges and deal with them compassionately and without compromising your values. Create the space, no matter how small, and begin your inner journey. If you are already on it, take it to the next level. Make more space, get a mentor who is aligned with your vision and shares your values. Do what you need to do to take the next leap.

As you focus on developing yourself to become more capable, resilient and creative, something magical will happen. This something magical was explained to me early on my path by my first coach, Daniel Priestley from Key Person Influence, with the simple analogy of a racing career.

A career in racing starts at the entry level with Go-Karts and as with all racing sports, racers start at the end of the startup line. Then they get better, win a few races, and eventually win the championship. Then they take a leap and move to Formula 3 where they start at the end of the line again. They win a few races, then the champions are faced with the next leap to Formula 1. This is similar in business and your inner journey. As you begin your mission, you may find that you fulfill your vision and move into the "next class" and all of a sudden, your current mission becomes trivial. The cool thing is that your confidence and attitude change about your current mission or business in a way that makes you really attractive. While you continue to fulfill that mission, you are no longer in need. You are not coming from a place of lack because you are now focusing on bigger things, bigger problems to solve, and bigger challenges to master. You have grown out of your mission and started a new part of your life. This is what happens when you bounce back and forth between inner and outer journeys. Everything falls into place and ties together like one beautiful symphony.

You can tell when something comes from your true purpose. This is when it creates such a strong impetus that you cannot think of anything else but getting it out into the world. So, you may have already begun formulating your Why, or if this is not new to you, let's dig a bit deeper. It's a lifelong journey after all, and it's necessary to check in regularly and delve ever deeper.

3

INTERNAL AND EXTERNAL WHY

"Always start with Why."

—Simon Sinek

ONE OF THE BIGGEST ISSUES I see with the wellness entrepreneurs I work with is that they do not tap deeply enough into their Why to find a unique position for their value and their business. Or they delve deeply while meditating or thinking but never actually write it down and make it approachable and understandable for the people around them. It is crucial that all content for your business comes from a place of purpose and deeper knowledge. This way you will be able to set yourself apart from others.

If you are "putting yourself out there" like everyone else does, it's almost impossible to avoid being compared on price. If you say you are a naturopath, new prospects will compare you to all the naturopaths they know or that they can find (through a Google search for instance). Your business will be competing with others around you.

However, if you say for instance, you are the Vitality Queen, people will have a hard time finding another one. Does Vitality Queen align with everyone? No. However, it aligns with the right ones. If you call yourself the Vitality Queen, you have a certain attitude toward what you do and how you do it. Most importantly, people with a similar attitude will be interested to hear more. Those are the ones you want to talk to and those are the ones who constitute your ideal clients.

At such a point, the only comparison those people will have for your service is the value you can give them and not a price point in comparison to another naturopath, because they don't go to a naturopath – they go to their Vitality Queen.

Make sense?

The most effective way to start finding your unique position is to dig deeply into your Why. This is because your uniqueness is made up of your story and the current environment you are in. I call that the internal and external Why. The internal Why is your story and the external Why is what has changed over the past ten years that makes your business relevant and possible now. The combination of the two is an expression of your individuality that has been uniquely formed during a specific time. There is no one else out there with the same experience, the same background, and, therefore, the same understanding of the world and everyone and everything in it. This needs to be the foundation of your business value proposition and all future creations to make it authentic, unique, and immensely powerful.

ACTIVITY #1

YOUR EXTERNAL WHY

"People run after what runs away from them and they want what they can't have."

—Oren Klaff

TRY TO THINK OF WHAT has changed over the past five to ten years that made your business possible. For example: "In the last decade, the Internet has grown rapidly and is still constantly changing the way we do business. It is now absolutely essential that small business owners learn how to position themselves effectively online." This is just a short part of the whole picture, but most people probably understand what I mean here. I have done extensive research on our daily habits and the numbers are amazing. Worldwide people use the internet over 6.5 hours every single day, over 500 hours of video content is uploaded to YouTube every minute, and almost 60 percent of the world's population are active social media users. [7, 8] I could talk passionately about this topic for hours, but that is beyond the scope of this book.

[7] "The Changing World of Digital in 2023," We Are Social, 26 Jan 2023, https://wearesocial.com/au/blog/2023/01/the-changing-world-of-digital-in-2023-2/.
[8] Eric Jhonsa, "How Much Could Google's YouTube Be Worth? Try More Than $100 Billion," The Street, May 12, 2018, https://www.thestreet.com/investing/youtube-might-be-worth-over-100-billion-14586599

The external Why is what connects with everyone. It's the bigger picture of what is happening in the world right now that everyone understands. So, whenever you do a speech or need to talk about what you do in some shape or form, starting with your external Why will get your audience to say, "Yes. We get that," from the very beginning. This approach will enable you to connect with your audience straight away, get it to listen to you so that you can communicate the content you want. It should only make up a very small proportion of your content, for example, five minutes of a thirty-minute speech. Another example for how you could express your Why that may make it a bit clearer is this: "Over the past decade, we have seen a massive increase in burnout and depression. More and more people suffer from high intensity jobs and the ever connectedness through technology, giving them no time for mindfulness and relaxation."

This tactic is something most people would understand. If you combine that with a few facts and figures underlining the issue, your audience will feel right away that this is a serious issue.

So, write down what has changed politically, socially, demographically, and economically in the past decade or more which would make people interested in your services now and what makes your business relevant. In other words, why is *now* the time for your business?

Research facts that complement and support your findings:

ACTIVITY #2

YOUR INTERNAL WHY

Now WE NEED TO DIG deeper because you need to find what drives you to do what you do. What are your vision, your mission, and your values? Only once you start living and making decisions based on your values and your Why will you truly find joy in your business.

Let's start by going back in time and writing down your story. Your story, particularly the highs and lows you have been through, is what will create the first strong emotional connection with your audience. The more you can show your vulnerability and really demonstrate the hardship and blessings you have experienced, the more you will connect with your audience.

Remember, people buy emotionally and they justify it logically. So, it's not so much about what you have done and when it happened but the real and raw stuff of life. Don't hold back when you start writing your story because you can always dial it down later. This is where courage comes in.

At a time when I hit rock bottom with my business, I decided to reach out to others and ask for help by sharing the truth of my situation. We often keep up appearances with our business. We want to show that everything is working, right? We wish to appear in control, but the truth is much more complex. It's common knowledge that there are ups and downs all the time.

So, I shared my situation: financial stress, a dearth of clients, and Christmas looming ahead. I felt like a complete loser. I reached out to people and shared how I felt on Facebook groups with business owners and coaches. The result was amazing. So many people got back to me and offered their help. Coaches who charged hundreds of dollars an hour offered their help and coached me to get me out of where I was.

Everyone has been through similar experiences in life, which means that they understand and because they understand, they want to help. It's the same with potential clients. They have been through the same or similar situations as you have and they will want to know more about how you overcame the challenges.

Writing down your story is best done by thinking about what happened about ten years ago that set you up to embark on the path. This is the path which led you to what happened five years ago, and then from there to what happened one year ago. Find three major events in your life that got you to where you are now. Times can obviously vary and the number of events is only a guideline. However, this will get you started.

What is your story?

10 years ago:

---

5 years ago:

_____

_____

_____

_____

_____

_____

_____

_____

_____

_____

1 year ago:

_____

_____

_____

_____

_____

_____

_____

_____

_____

_____

_____

One episode should lead into another, and the end result is what you currently do for a living. For example, in my case, I provide a fully comprehensive program for wellness entrepreneurs. Tap into the emotions of the struggles you've faced and the successes you've achieved.

Writing down your external and internal Why(s) should help clear your perception of your big vision. Your vision and mission are what get you up in the morning. They are your overall life goal. You might not get it right at first but it's a process. Let's write something down. You can always change it later. Mine, for example, changed five years ago. I always wanted to become a General Manager of a Grand Five-Star Hotel, but that goal wasn't right for me. I felt another calling. Now, my vision is to "co-create 100,000 impactful wellness entrepreneurs and move the world to sustainable wellness."

What's yours?

My vision is

_____

_____

_____

_____

_____

_____

With a strong vision comes the desire to change things and next comes how you want to change people. As I mentioned in the beginning of this part of the book, you can't change others, only yourself. Once you have defined your vision, mission, and values, before you try to go out there and change the world, let me share with you a few more things that I have experienced to help you along the way.

4

SELF LOVE AND
UNCONDITIONAL LOVE

*"Owning our story and loving ourselves through that process is
the bravest thing that we'll ever do."*

—Brené Brown

WHEN I CAME BACK to Australia after traveling through Europe for four years, a whole new world opened up to me. I learned about alternative therapies, preventative health, and how lifestyle changes can have a massive impact on our health. From energy healing to osteopathy, listening and art therapy to numerology and spiritual healing, the list went on.

There was an essential core value to all these holistic health practices which I only understood much later. All of them had one thing in common and that was putting yourself first, tuning in with who you truly are. One might also call this self-love. There is a beautiful speech about Loving Oneself which was falsely claimed to be Charlie Chaplin's seventieth birthday speech and supposedly a resumé of his life and philosophy. In fact, it was written after his death by an American author, Kim McMillen. It reveals much in its simplicity and beauty.

As I began to love myself...

I found that anguish and emotional suffering are only warning signs that I was living against my own truth.

Today, I know, this is 'AUTHENTICITY'.

As I began to love myself, I understood how much it can offend somebody as I try to force my desires on this person, even though I knew the time was not right and the person was not ready for it, and even though this person was me.

Today I call it 'RESPECT'.

As I began to love myself, I stopped craving for a different life, and I could see that everything that surrounded me was inviting me to grow. Today I call it 'MATURITY'.

As I began to love myself, I understood that under any circumstance, I am in the right place at the right time, and everything happens at the exactly right moment, so I could be calm.

Today I call it 'SELF-CONFIDENCE'.

As I began to love myself, I quit stealing my own time, and I stopped designing huge projects for the future. Today, I only do what brings me joy and happiness, things I love to do and that make my heart cheer, and I do them in my own way and in my own rhythm.

Today I call it 'SIMPLICITY'.

As I began to love myself, I freed myself of anything that is no good for my health — food, people, things, situations, and everything that drew me down and away from myself. At first, I called this attitude a healthy egoism.

Today I know it is 'LOVE OF ONESELF'.

As I mentioned above, I only understood this idea much later. However, through my work with holistic practitioners, I learned and experienced methodologies, practices, and technology that were mind-blowing. All I wanted was to tell my family about all these new things. I was so excited and was looking forward to sharing it all so that they could change their lives.

I booked flights a year later and went back to Germany for a holiday and visited my family. Remember the priest? What do you think happened when I sat down with my family and told them about all those new and amazing, life-changing experiences?

You probably guessed right. All I received was resistance. "That's nice but that won't work for me," and "That's all good but it's not the right time at the moment." These are some of the things that we all probably know only too well. In some cases, I was even ridiculed for my plant-based diet. It's one thing talking with someone who is stubborn and not open to change, but it hurts deeply being laughed at by your family and friends for your lifestyle choices while you can clearly see they are suffering or will suffer.

Family is everything for me. What is there in life without your family and friends? Between the ages of four and nine, I lived alone with my mother, who was shunned by the village because she had left my father, the local priest's son. Of course, in the people's eyes, she had to be the source of the divorce, not him. It was a hard time for my mother. She was working a lot to keep her head above the water and I spent a lot of time with my grandparents. My mother also talked to me about the challenges she faced every day because she didn't have anyone else to talk with.

I believe that this part of my life created an immensely strong bond between my mother and me, and equally with my grandparents. It taught me the importance of family. I can't express in words how much I love my family. My eyes fill with tears as I write this. Seeing them suffer is the worst torture I could imagine.

With what I have learned, I understood that much of their suffering in the areas of health, physicality, mentality, and spirituality had been brought upon themselves. That hurt even more. My will was strong to change their behavior and I focused on their pain when I first came back. From that pain I expressed what I wanted for them. The reaction reflected how I expressed myself. "Don't worry about us, my son. Just focus on your life and make sure that you are safe."

My frustration was palpable, and I couldn't understand them. I left disappointed and returned to Australia. Back then, I didn't understand what was going on. All I wanted to do was help. Their lives could have been so much better, I thought to myself.

But as in our story about the priest, that is not how it works. If you try to push change on people, they will naturally resist. It's simply how we are wired after thousands of years of evolution. When we were living in caves, a change in our environment seldom meant anything good. We would come back to our camp and see that things had been disturbed like the tools or places to sit or sleep. This would probably have been caused by an animal, most likely a predator. So, when we see change, we fear it and therefore try to avoid it.

This fear reaction might have served us thousands of years ago, but change is constant in our current world. In fact, probably the only constant thing in life is change. The online world can be so fast that we feel we are constantly playing catch up. That's a change we need to embrace to benefit from it. With personal relationships, I realize that we can't expect others to embrace the change we want them to make. This expectation will impact our relationships badly and it will more likely distance us from others than forge stronger relationships, which are the basis for trust and real change.

After visiting my family that year, I went on a journey of self-development and conscious living. I stepped back from the impulse to change my family. Being on the other side of the world helped me and I guess I needed the space to learn to focus on myself and become a bigger man before going back. I had many small and big breakthroughs on that journey, both spiritually and in terms of mindset. The mindset needs to be one of pure love.

Two years later, I went back to my family again, but this time I had the intention to go back with pure, unconditional love. I said to myself that all I wanted was to have a wonderful time with my family and close friends without wanting to change anybody. I was content within myself and had discovered that I needed to focus on what was best for me. Exactly what my family suggested. Lightbulb moment! Interesting how life goes, isn't it? I discovered a new love for myself, my journey and, most importantly, where I come from.

My holiday to Europe, following this lightbulb moment, was the best holiday with my family and friends that I ever had. I spent lots of quality time with the people who were the closest to me. A few days before we left to come back to Australia, something special happened.

Without having planned it, I sat at the breakfast table with my mother and father and they started to ask about my journey, my life-style, and what I had learned. They saw me happy and healthy and wanted to know what I was doing. There was also no pressure from me and I truly believe that if you live your values and stay true to your authentic self, people get curious. The next two hours we talked about my plant-based lifestyle and all the different therapies that I learned about through my work.

Now my mother looks for alternative solutions to her health problems and doesn't just pop a pill. By going to my family with uncon-ditional love and no expectations, I planted a seed which is now starting to sprout. Or maybe the seed was already there and I helped nurture it. It doesn't matter. I think this is the way to prosperity and harmony, plant-ing good seeds for change and nurturing the seeds we want to thrive. The rest needs to emerge. Isn't that true nature? Planting a seed with love, nurturing that seed and new life, and then letting go to let things happen as they are meant to? We can guide and nurture by reminding the people around us what is possible through our actions and not try to mold people into forms or to prevent the struggles and difficulties they may face. In fact, letting the wheels fall off now and then and letting people make their own mistakes will make them stronger. We can provide a safe space for ourselves and others to make that growth happen. It's the difference between a natural, organic approach that is dynamic and balanced versus the forced, engineered creation that ignores the environment or the space and often does the job crudely and inefficiently. The latter gives the illusion of control but is ultimately bound to fail. Make the mistakes, let the wheels fall off, and practice to make the space in your life to check in with yourself because, as long as we take care of ourselves and live our values, we can plant and nurture the seeds of positive change.

You need to put yourself first. To love yourself is an essential part of your inner journey or the Inner Game you need to play so you can find your vision, your Why and how you can make an impact in the world that is germane to you.

With self-love, we can be content within and be the change we want to see in the world. That's it. Self-love sounds simple if we put it like that, but it's certainly not easy or, in fact, a finite journey. And in some ways, when you take away your need to change someone else, life becomes easier.

It takes practice to truly become aware of yourself and be able to live a life from a place of joy and contentment. In the end, self-love and putting yourself first come down to taking responsibility for yourself.

5

RESPONSIBILITY

"It is the set of the sails, not the direction of the wind which determines which way we will go."

—Jim Rohn

TO GROW AND BECOME a better person, we have to take things into our own hands. We can't blame circumstances or others for our situation. So, learn how to set your sails no matter the circumstances.

To me, taking responsibility for your life means making choices and often without knowing all the answers. So many people live in fear of the unknown, of losing face or disappointing others, without the courage to take action in spite of it. Following your dreams towards a life of fulfillment, purpose, and joy comes with the risk of losing, failing, or disappointing others.

I remember when it came to the point in my life to listen to the nudges the universe was giving me. It was said in one of the books that were put into my pathway: "Think about what your grandfather would say who has been through war, maybe lost his family, friends and his home and you would tell him that you will not pursue your dreams because you fear losing a bit of money."

This hit home for me big time. I lost my grandfather in the year when my life was in turmoil and when I changed everything. My grandfather had to flee Prussia in the Second World War, lost his parents and brothers to the war, and then ended up in East Germany where he could never rise to all the aspirations and dreams he had. He was stuck under the Communist regime and all the oppression that came with it.

I saw him being dedicated, almost obsessive with his work. Everyone in the local area knew he was the best at what he did. But none of that made much difference in creating abundance or fulfillment of his dreams.

I think he felt stuck because my grandmother was frequently sick and he couldn't take her to West Germany to provide the life he wanted for her. The East German communist system held him back and he couldn't do anything about it. He knew exactly why it was not working – like so many others as well – but his drive was strong and his inner voice was loud. Like a lion that has been held captive for too long, he started to decline. He became embittered and moved to alcohol and cigarettes. In the end, cancer took him.

In the western world, we have a safety net and much more choice now! Yes, you may have to feed a family, put your kids through school, take care of a friend in need or whatever the situation is, but you still have a choice. My grandfather did too, but the risk of trying to cross the border with my sick grandmother was a risk of life and death.

All of that made me think about that quote from the book I was reading and I thought, I have to take responsibility for my life and make the choice to move toward my dreams. Nothing could happen to me. There wasn't a big wall with armed guards and dogs watching 24/7. There wasn't an oppressive, communist regime that separated me from a better life. There wasn't anything to lose. In the western world, if you are willing to work, there will always be a safety net.

It's not like in developing countries, where one might starve or miss needed medical attention. In the event of failure, I would not face a death sentence like my grandfather had.

No matter where you are in life, if you have kids or not, own a house or pay rent, have a fancy car or use public transport, how happy are you really? Is what you do making you finish work each day and think, "Yes, I worked toward my dreams and purpose and at the same time I had fun with it"?

Stop letting fear get in the way. Fear is natural but have the courage to make choices that are in alignment with your purpose and dreams no matter the risk.

I remember a great networking event which embodied the energy around choice and living life to the fullest. The main presenter on stage was full of vibrant energy, filling the room with excitement. He talked about making the most of life every single day. He had millions of dollars and, for him, life was not about buying stuff but experiencing every moment at its fullest. "SQUEEEZE THE JUUUUUIIIICE," he screamed into the microphone.

I will never forget that feeling he instilled in me back then. That feeling of getting everything you can out of every day, every minute and every second of life, comes from living a life of purpose, taking risks to move forward in the direction your heart tells you to go. Yes, there will be hardship but it's necessary for you to grow. There is no way around it. The other way is to stay where you are and try to be comfortable, but my experience shows that that doesn't last long either. I believe life is our soul's journey to grow and have an experience so rich with all facets of joy and sorrow that it comes out with an unimaginable muchness on the other side.

Let's "squeeze the juice" together! Strip ourselves of the fears and stories we make up in our heads and live a life of purpose through growing our business and self. It's time to take responsibility for our life, the planet, future generations, and that same self-responsibility when it comes to our marketing, sales, and business growth. For this is what you need to do to plant the seed, become a bigger person and make a dent in the world!

6

OVERCOMING ONE'S FEARS

"The meaning of life is to find your gift and the purpose of life is to give it away."

—Picasso

MY LIFE'S GIFT IS MY PASSION and I believe everyone's passion is their life's gift. The more ways we find to share our gift with as many people as we can, the closer we live to our life's purpose. If you use your passion to make someone's life better or even transform it, you will experience an exhilarating, almost addictive, feeling of gratitude and pleasure. It will make you happy. This feeling of gratefulness is one of the most rewarding things in life.

I know your passion is what you do. That's why you are on the pathway to becoming an influential wellness entrepreneur; or you may consider yourself already influential and now you want to take it to the next level. No matter how you see yourself, in order to live your life's purpose and achieve what you seek, you need to shed your fears of judgment and rejection so you can truly become who you are supposed to be and help as many people as possible.

Your business success will derive from a combination of your Inner Game which includes self-love, your Why, overcoming your fears, and your Outer Game including implementing the right business strategies, systems, and tools which we will discuss in the second half of this book. In other words, continuing to stay in your comfort zone, selling time for money, and relying on word of mouth will not enable you to get your passion out to the world. As someone famously said, "Insanity is doing the same thing over and over again and expecting different results."

Don't get me wrong. It's not about becoming a world Wellness Leader traveling the world if that is not your thing. I have seen and worked with many local practitioners who are great influencers and change-makers in their local community. "Playing the game" according to your values and vision will make you a part of that beautiful movement toward sustainable wellness. There will be many helpful tools and strategies in this book that will support your wellness business journey no matter how you want to do this. I encourage you to take it as far as you can. Like everything in nature, you grow as tall as you can. I have never heard a tree say, "I am okay with this height. I shall stop here."

My passion is to lift your game up to the next level and not only help you to create an abundant life but also impact the health and well-being of millions of people around the world.

I know if I help you to make a global impact, I will help hundreds or thousands of people transform their lives through you.

To do that, I know that one of the biggest hurdles for you is to face your fear of failure, rejection, and judgment. It's the same for everyone.

I have seen many practitioners create online programs and new ways to deliver their transformational knowledge online on a greater scale, only to see them falter at the end because they thought it wasn't perfect yet or didn't provide the level of value, knowledge, and expertise they intended.

It is not about creating something perfect for months and months in a closed room. That approach in itself is flawed because the paradox of perfectionism is that you can only make something perfect if you are getting it done in the first place. Only if you have created something in the first place, do you have the chance to improve your creation and raise it to perfection.

Of course, your creation will never be perfect but the point is that if you don't create something and get it out to others, your idea will wither on the vine. If you don't get it out there, you fail, but if you get it out there, you may experience some kind of failure because it's not perfect. Failure will always be part of the journey. This knowledge does not make it easier but it certainly helps to overcome your fear, hesitation, and procrastination. Everything you see around you that you may compare yourself to has been built, failed, and improved continuously to the point that you now compare yourself to it. Every creator had those fears and made up stories in their head that, had they listened to them, they would have stopped the creation entirely. There is no growth without struggle. No matter how much we seek comfort and happiness, life doesn't work like that. Life is like a rollercoaster; it goes up and down but not on a straight rail without curves and bumps. The trick is to ride it and pull your courage from deep within you when it comes to the parts that you fear.

If you think about it, it's a really crazy situation. Every time you face something new or different, your brain imagines the worst scenario possible and then hits "repeat". I think that this fear will never fully disappear. We learn to deal with it and "do it anyway". I work on that every day by meditating and checking in with myself throughout the day. You can't rely only on your courage. The drive has to come from within, from a place that is true. If not, your courage will be random and you'll say yes to everything no matter what. Fear is a guide and you have to find when to use your courage and when to flow around the obstacle.

So, what can we do to overcome this hurdle?

The first thing that always helps is to be truthful. Tell people that you created your new program, modality, video, speech, whatever it is for the first time and that you are nervous about how it will turn out.

This will do two things. Your audience understands that what's to come will not be perfect and mistakes are likely, although most of the time they stay unnoticed anyway. That sets the right expectations and all the things that will go wrong won't really matter. They will focus on what actually matters: your content and the value you share.

The second thing is that you will be calmer and your nervousness will diminish because you shared what you felt; there is no hiding or pretending anymore. It's out, everybody knows you are not perfect and are completely human. The crowd will love you for that and so will your body and mind.

You can do pilot programs for a discounted price, test versions for free, beta-phase for selected people, and so forth. As long as you set the expectations right, you have nothing to fear.

People actually like to be part of creating something and will feel good about helping you to get started and to provide feedback. Little "tricks" like that will get you started and put you into action. Once you set a date, sell a program, apply for that speaking gig, and so forth, you are committed.

After you have experienced loving feedback from others and see that your worst fears never materialized, you will have more confidence every time.

Always being upfront with how you feel and what your struggles are is being authentic. It's not helpful to stay inactive because "you are not feeling it" and that attitude is also not authentic. Don't wait to feel great about something that you think is scary or daunting in some shape or form. This will only hold you back and you will probably never do it. Instead, remember why you do what you do and that the right things will come to you as you stay true to yourself and your values. That's authenticity, and that's how you work with your fears to become a better version of yourself.

Another great part of this is its simplicity in leading to action.

7

ASKING THE RIGHT QUESTIONS

"You are the average of the five people you spend the most time with."

—Jim Rhon

I REMEMBER MY FIRST course about entrepreneurship outside of university. I learned some principles of business that I still use today and received one of the best pieces of advice ever.

Whenever I hear something new, I soak it up like a sponge, go home and think about how I can implement it in what I do. This is one of my great gifts and I am very grateful for it. It is easy for me to find value in what other people say and I can easily put myself in other people's shoes.

I also always quickly figure out what I want to achieve with this knowledge and set new goals. This is not common. Not all people function in the same way. Some people may take longer to pick up information which often leaves them feeling overwhelmed. New information, specifically if it is information that suggests making changes, is hard to take on sometimes. Setting new goals based on new information is even harder. As discussed earlier, we have a natural resistance to change and are more programmed for sameness.

Before I received this valuable advice on how to avoid feeling over-whelmed, I often got stuck in my head and most of the time never started anything that excited me.

After we set new goals, we ponder how to achieve them. What are the major milestones to achieve the goal? And what of the little steps in between? I attended a great talk by a business buddy of mine who has worked in corporate as a business coach for over twenty years, and he talked about how only a very few people take the time to actually plan out their goals, which creates massive procrastination. If we set a big goal, it's easy to get overwhelmed. In fact, statistics show that only one percent or less achieve the goals they set for themselves.

Success is not about whether you can achieve the big goal you set for yourself. It's about whether you believe you can do the little steps toward the milestones of that goal. If you know the small steps, you can chip away at them, each one at a time. Then progress is simply about keeping going. However, you need to get clear on what those steps are and that is a challenge. It takes time and you will surely run into hurdles.

Whenever I set a new goal for myself before I got this valuable advice, the more I planned out those little steps, the more "how's" seemed to come up so that I had no idea how to progress. Sometimes it was little things like how to set up an online calendar or create an email automation, but there were also bigger questions like how do I convert a lead into a sale now that I have a new way of generating leads. One question leads into another. Sometimes I thought about it for weeks, desperately trying to figure it out.

After a while, life got in the way again – a new project, a long-planned holiday, a family emergency – you know how it goes. After that, the new goal was very distant and it simply seemed too hard.

The same can happen with your decision to do a beta version of an online course or a monthly workshop you always wanted to do. You may overcome the initial fear and hesitation, set the date, and even start writing some content.

Then you realize you need to set up a landing page, sell tickets online, have a membership area on your website, handle all the marketing, and so on. All of a sudden, you find yourself opening the fridge for the seventh time to check what's for dinner. Procrastination kicks in.

You find other tasks that you do first. "If I get this done first, I will get the other thing done." You put off the wrong job. The one task that you were excited about is what you de-prioritize. But you are always aware of it, and, every time you work on something different, you think about it. And then you do something else that is supposed to be a great success in your business and the same cycle happens again, and so on and so on. This is the process of becoming overwhelmed. There are all manner of things that you could do that turn into "you should do". You are not focused and clear in your tasks. Everything becomes kind of muddy and you start to cope rather than thrive with confidence. This, of course, affects everything, not only your business. Your family feels you are stressed, your friends notice something is not quite right, and all of a sudden you are sick in bed because you didn't take care of yourself. I used to get sick close to ten times a year during the worst cycles of my business life. It was so frustrating. I beat myself up for not taking care of myself and that, in turn, as you may have guessed, made everything worse.

In this state, you lose all momentum and creativity. The initially exciting task feels like a chore and you are not one with the Fun and Flow of your business anymore. There is no longer much energy in what you do and this dramatically affects your creativity. You think to yourself, "What happened? How did I get from having all that drive and enthusiasm to this?" Feeling perplexed happens to all of us, and the only way I found to overcome this is following that advice I mentioned earlier about how to pursue goals.

Now here is the piece of advice that I have been given which will solve all these problems:

... drum roll ...

... more drum roll ...

... sorry for being silly ...

... not really ...

… Ok here it comes:

Don't ask yourself HOW but WHO!

Who has done this before? Who is an expert in this particular field? Who has been there, done that? Or simply, who always lifts me up or has a different perspective of situations than I do?

Once you find that person, contact them and ask for help. You wouldn't believe what can happen. I had business coaches giving me free advice for weeks when they would normally charge hundreds of dollars per hour. Others simply did stuff for me for free, like setting up my domain or scheduling my social media on a new platform.

You see, here is the reality: All of these coaches are, in fact, business owners who have been where you are. They know how hard it is and how much difference a little bit of help can really make. I mean, think about it: If I asked you right now if you would be willing to have a ten-minute conversation with me about a problem that I have in my life, which your expertise could help with, what would you say?

That's right. In the end, we are all in business to help people. So yes, if you ask for help, you will get it. But you have to ask!

I solved so many problems with a quick ten-minute phone call that would usually have taken me days or weeks to solve, or that I simply would have given up on solving. Again, this is overcoming our fears. We imagine that others are too busy or too important to talk to us. But that's not the case. Yes, they are busy, but the worst thing that can happen is being told to call another time.

All of that is a small hurdle to overcome compared to losing all your momentum and procrastinating to the point that the fridge is more interesting than getting things done. Don't get me wrong – I love food – but you know what I mean. It is so critical to get out of your own head. We naturally want to make things perfect as business owners and we get hung up on the details. You need to find ways to step back, far back, like hovering over your business to get a bird's-eye view. My experience shows that the quickest and easiest way to achieve success is to get a different perspective, ideally from those people who have been in your situation and are experts in what they do. They will tell you what to do now and what to tackle later. I even had people offering to follow up with me to keep me accountable. And you can do the same for them. Don't underestimate your own value. You have a lot to offer. Just ask what you can do for them. Over time, you'll discover what different people need and you can get specific about what you can offer them.

Think about the other side. How do you feel when someone asks you for help? Do you feel good? Maybe even a bit important? Of course, the truth is that you are. We all are. So, let's keep that in mind when we run into a problem. Most people don't want anything in return when you ask kindly and genuinely, but keep in mind that you have a lot to give as well so there is always the opportunity to give back. You can even swap services at a later point. Know this and go in there confidently, sharing your truth and speaking from the heart. There is a sort of magic in this attitude and collaborative mindset.

The best result of such conversations is the relationships that often come out of them. By opening up and showing that you are human and vulnerable, other people will do the same and open up too, especially those people whom we think are truly successful.

I have created beautiful relationships by reaching out and asking for help, relationships that went much further than the help I asked for and brought tremendous value to my life and business.

Don't underestimate the power of asking.

I once did a shout-out in a closed Facebook group of entrepreneurs saying that I needed help with my business because it was not going well and I felt stuck, had no money, and didn't know how to get out from under my problems. The help I received was amazing. I got free business coaching and one of the people even offered me a part-time consulting job that enabled me to earn enough money to tide me over that bad patch. That alone was remarkable, but I also made an excellent friend from it.

To this day, we talk about business to lift each other up or simply to vent some things we wouldn't share with others because we have built great trust between us. All of this started with me opening up and sharing my truth.

In the end, what will lift your business to new heights is the people you surround yourself with. One of my favorite motivational speakers, Jim Rohn, said, "You are the average of the five people you spend the most time with." We all know the importance of friendships and strong bonds with others. Being in business is a great way to isolate yourself. You need to find ways to counteract that.

In Germany, children and their parents have to make a decision in the fourth grade, when children are ten or eleven years old, about whether to attend high school (more specifically, an academic education) or a trade-oriented school. That is very early to make a decision like that. I was told that I had the potential but needed to work harder to make it into high school. It was the time of my adoption and I had no idea what to do. The only reason I decided to go to high school was because my best friend was going there and I didn't want us to be separated.

Even if you have a hard time, friends and relationships will keep you going in the right direction, but these must be friends who are going in the direction you envision. You need to decide who those people are and make an effort to build a relationship with them. Through this effort, you will keep moving toward your purpose and experience the joy and happiness that comes with it.

Forming collaborative relationships is the best way to keep momentum in your business and stay productive. These relationships lift you up and provide invaluable input. Yes, we often don't feel like putting in the effort to develop these relationships and we may think we risk letting others down. Don't let that get in the way. That story is only in your head.

Every time I asked for help and reached out to others, I got back into flow, increased my energy levels and, most importantly, inculcated a renewed belief in what I do and who I am.

Imagine what could happen to your business and life if you could get over yourself and ask for help when a problem arises. If you want fun and flow in your business and life, genuine "from the heart" communication is everything!

Never underestimate the power of asking. Don't ask HOW, ask WHO!

Taking this to another level: What could happen to your business if you asked two new people every day if they want YOUR help? But more about that later.

8

SELF-DOUBT

"If you hear a voice within you say you cannot paint, then by all means paint and that voice will be silenced."

—Vincent Van Gogh

THIS BOOK IS ABOUT GIVING you my insight from the past ten years and my growth from a young adult who didn't know what to do with his life to finding the love of my life and running my own business on the other side of the planet. On this journey, self-doubt was a constant companion, popping up every time I made a new choice. Making choices that your social circle will disapprove is going to be part of your business journey one way or another, so it's important that we discuss acting in spite of self-doubt.

From 2014 to 2016, I lived with the love of my life Teresa in Vienna, right next to the Schönbrunn Palace gardens. Every morning, I went for a run amongst those beautiful trees, carefully kept gardens, sculptures, and decadent buildings (including the world's first zoo, incidentally). It was amazing.

I worked for a startup business while we built websites for Australian and Austrian businesses. We went to the city often, using a car-sharing service that only had BMWs and Mini Convertibles. Imagine driving through Vienna with the roof down, seeing all the beautiful buildings and stopping in the nearby wine hills for a picnic. Life was good.

As life ticked along, I felt something missing – a small trickle of doubt that Vienna was really the right place for us. I started to explore that feeling, trying to figure out why it was growing inside me. After a while, Teresa and I noticed that we found it really hard to find friends and be part of a community. That was the first problem. In hindsight, I think if you move around a lot, finding friends and communities in cities is hard anywhere. However, at the time we started to feel isolated even though we went to networking events, looked up expat activities to join and lived pretty centrally. Another, probably more significant issue at the time, was something commonly known as *Freunderlwirtschaft*, which means "Friends Economy". This meant that most business contracts were handed from friend to friend or kept within the family. It was almost impossible to get business locally without being at least introduced by someone. We started to do projects for free to build trust but that wasn't sustainable because it took too long to get paid work afterwards.

This often left us frustrated. One time, we wrote a proposal as a counteroffer to another business. We knew our offer was lower in price and included more value, but we received a response telling us that they went with the other guys because their cousin recommended them. That was literally their only reason. Now I also understand that we could have handled the situation differently. A year later, I would receive some good advice: "never send a proposal" (that is, always present it in person). From that point onward, I never sent a proposal before having had a deep conversation with the client to make a personal connection. More on that in the second half of this book. The point here is that we reflected on our work, thinking that it might not be good enough, that WE might not be good enough. Here was the little self-doubt monster that we constantly had to keep in check, even as it grew and grew.

I believe that, when we get rejected or people disapprove of us, self-doubt creeps in very quickly, even when we are given a reason that has nothing to do with us. I am someone who is very self-critical and I will always look at how I can improve myself, examine how I do things, and never blame others, but that process makes doubting yourself really easy. Self-doubt can really throw you off track and add to the feeling of being overwhelmed, but it can also be a big driver. All entrepreneurs and business owners talk about this dynamic. Comparing yourself with others and doubting yourself is something they all struggle with and, depending on how far they are on their business journey, they experience this on different levels. Dealing with self-doubt is now very different for me compared to my time in Vienna. The little self-doubt monster never dies but it can be a driver that moves you forward, as much as it can be a weight that holds you back.

We kept telling ourselves that the success of our business needed time and that the life we were living in Vienna was beautiful. Funnily enough, the way we make up negative stories is akin to positive stories in the sense that we are trying to justify our decisions logically. We could clearly feel that things were not quite right, but we focused on why we got to Vienna in the first place and justified our decisions with that. As we continued to struggle to get work with our business, I started to look for jobs in my old profession in hospitality. As it turned out, I was overqualified for my old position as a receptionist and not committed to the job for long enough for higher level management positions.

BOOM! There was another self-doubt bomb. I always thought I could fall back to hospitality quickly and with ease. Slowly but surely, self-doubt started to eat my confidence in business and neither the palace gardens of Schönbrunn nor the beauty of ice skating in front of the old parliament house could overcome that. I started to get unhappier and increasingly frustrated.

Near the end of our Vienna episode, I received a grant from the German government which allowed me to work for an Austrian startup.

It was given so that I could learn from the experience, understand the culture, and use this for my own business. The experience I had was not what I imagined but again, in hindsight, probably exactly what we needed to push us to take the next big step. I spent most of my time doing the marketing for that business because they lacked the resources to hire someone. The owner took me to different business events and introduced me to the "big guys". Unfortunately, I didn't like these events. They simply didn't feel right. The people he introduced me to felt pretentious, overly polite, and unapproachable. I saw my companion walking and talking with joy and making connections. And what of myself? Now I look back and see the self-doubt and lack of confidence that filled me. Coming from a tiny village, all of this socializing felt out of my league. Back then, I felt angry and resentful. Now, I see that I was not ready as a person. This is why the Inner Game is so important. It's never about the others. It's always about you growing into the person you need to be to handle the ever-growing challenges on your journey so that you can make better decisions. Self-doubt is one of the hurdles that will always be with you.

This lack of community and what we saw as closed-mindedness quickly started to rub us the wrong way, so we decided to leave and make a big change. We spent a while in an exploratory phase but, as ever, opportunity finds you when you are ready for it. When we finally made the firm decision to move, we quickly found an opportunity to run a bed-and-breakfast in France through a house-sitting website. We had both studied hospitality and loved the thought of living in rural France for a while so we just went for it. This was how we lived our lives. If something didn't suit us, we changed, no matter how unknown and scary the future looked! This is something that Teresa taught me. If you don't like something, change it. Nobody is forcing you to stay in a place or hang out with certain people. You are the master of your life; there is always a choice.

My family thought we were completely nuts, though. They thought giving up a good life in Vienna to do something completely different in a country where we didn't even speak the language was crazy. On the contrary, we thought living a life in a place where you were not happy was crazy and learning a language was not a big deal. My mother tongue is German and I am writing this book in English!

The self-doubt that came with the comments from my family was strong as you can imagine. People would always say things that created doubt, but by the time that happened, the decision had already been made. I learned to trust what felt right in the moment and make a decision. You decide something based on more than your intellect. You make a decision based on how you live your life and who you are as an individual, a decision made from the inside out. You are moving faster than self-doubt. I think that most of the time when people tell you that you can't do something, it's because they doubt themselves the most. They think they can't do it, so they tell you that you can't either. Because if you do it, that means that they probably could have too and they can no longer blame circumstances. That doesn't mean you should ignore valuable advice from others because it's important to listen to mentors and people you admire. But if something doesn't feel right, and you want to change it, don't let small-mindedness and fear of others and yourself get in the way. It is about moving faster than self-doubt, not moving faster than well-founded reason and the wisdom of experienced and like-minded people.

We make up self-doubt stories in our mind when it comes to doing new things or changing the way we do them. Our brain is wired like that. "Make up the worst possible scenario and then hit *Repeat.*" I said this before but it is one of the biggest lessons that I remind myself of because these stories never come true. I made so many decisions that were judged to be "crazy" by others and never even one of the stories came true. In fact, most of the time the opposite happened and I experienced something I would never want to have missed.

I truly want you to become an influential wellness entrepreneur and make a global impact but you have to give yourself the "green light". You have to simply GO FOR IT. Through self-love, you can take full responsibility for your life and business and overcome your fears. Then you can start moving faster than your brain can think up all those self-doubting thoughts.

It doesn't matter if you have one person, three or fifteen in your newly developed wellness program or whether you think your service is up to the standard. You just have to go with it. You have to give yourself a "green light" and start moving. Don't fall back on what is comfortable for you. Decide what you want to do and then pursue it. Outline the steps, set the dates, make the entries in your calendar, and stick to the program. Don't beat yourself up if you can't make a deadline, because this regimen is more about moving toward a direction that's right for you than arriving in time.

One item I like to have on my white board in my office – where I can see it every day – is a table with four columns: day, week, month, and ninety days. Every quarter, I decide what is that new goal or intention I want to achieve over the next ninety days. Then, it is absolutely crucial to do something that gets me closer to my vision. I always think, "What do I need to do to move the world to sustainable wellness?" Once I find my ninety-day goal, I work backward to decide what the three major milestones or subgoals are that I need to achieve each month. Sometimes, I only think about what I can achieve in one month on this road and put that in the third column without thinking about the other monthly steps. As I said previously, time is not that important; a ninety-day goal can stay for another cycle or two. To succeed within the ninety days is only crucial if your number one goal is financial success, but since you are still reading, I would say we are on the same page here. The next step is to figure out what you need to do for the week to move toward your monthly goal and after that to set out three things that you want to do for the day that will help you achieve your weekly goals. The daily to-dos are a bit fluid because sometimes they are subsumed in the business activities, but I always have the intention to find three things that are moving me toward my weekly, monthly, and therefore ninety-day goal.

Day	Week	Month (insert current month)	90 Days (insert current month and end of quarter month)
Daily to-do's	Weekly Goal	Monthly Goal	Goal and intention to achieve your vision

Sometimes new goals or projects start slowly and that's fine, too. For example, when I developed my first coaching program, it was designed to be a group program. This way I could leverage my time and get people to collaborate among themselves. We will discuss how to create programs and get others involved later in the book.

When I first started, I got one person signed up and she was mostly interested in getting a new website. This was still what we were known for and also what felt most comfortable to us. Naturally in the beginning, we would fall back on building websites when pitching our new program idea. But I went for it anyway. We built the website but we also followed and refined our new program. From there, we grew to having a dozen people in a fully scalable program at $1,000 per person a month.

I often think that business is a fine balance between being positive, delusional, self-doubting, and overwhelmed. We have to surpass self-doubt but we also can't make irrational decisions. Business decisions need to be calculated and the pros and cons of new opportunities need to be assessed because, once you move fast and are in flow, it's more choosing between existing opportunities than trying to find a new one. Ignore the stories in your head, find ways to stay on track, and remind yourself why you are doing what you do.

Even if your program isn't perfect (you may only have one person signed up for your group program), it's still worth doing it because getting someone to commit to go all the way creates a win-win for all parties involved. On top of that, you are on a pathway of creating a different and more abundant life for yourself, your family, and your clients.

We started our business by building websites for any small business owner. They came to us saying that they wanted a new website, but we dug deeper into what they wanted. It was clear that they were trying to get more people through the door and grow their business. Of course. We told them that a website alone wouldn't do that. There are many other matters you have to consider, such as SEO (Search Engine Optimization), social media, email marketing, directory listings, and so forth. You have to create a complete online presence that provides many touchpoints for your prospects to experience your business. All of these touchpoints have to be congruent too.

They would say, "Yes, we understand, but let's do the website first." With our naive, youthful enthusiasm (and the desperate need for money), we said yes and built the websites. I had the feeling it might not be the right way to go about it, but back then I frequently doubted my inner voice. Once we finished the websites, we asked if we should now start working on all the other factors we talked about and the answer usually was: "No, not yet, we are happy with the website and don't have the time and money to invest more into this." Three or six months later, they would get back to us asking why their website still wasn't getting them any new clients. "Weeeeell," we said, "we told you so." We didn't really, but you can see what happened there.

See, it went like having a practice and selling one's expertise on a session-by-session basis. The session is something people come in for to get one fix because they think that's what they need to get rid of their problems, like our clients did with their websites. However, you know they need several sessions to make lifestyle changes to really resolve the underlying issues and create well-being. Often as business owners or service providers, we can see what lies ahead for our clients even when they can't.

A session-by-session approach is about fixing people and a program is about empowering them. However, doing sessions means facing two major problems.

First of all, it's a bit like having to sell yourself, which makes selling hard and uncomfortable. This is probably the number one reason why many practitioners pay lots of money for rent in a clinic: the clinic will take care of you and funnel people through. This, of course, makes you completely reliant on that clinic and the usually high costs for rent.

Secondly, you leave a lot of money on the table. In fact, about 40 percent on average. Why? Maybe this scenario sounds familiar: A new referral comes in for their first consultation and you have a nice chat, you assess the issue and determine how you can help. Considering what you learned, you estimate that you would need about ten sessions to address the issue. The client asks you how long it will take to fix this. Now trying to "fix" people is another problem in itself but let's focus on the money issue. You tell the client that it depends but probably will be between six to ten sessions. You don't want to put them off by telling them that it will definitely be ten sessions and it's $120 per session. I often see price-reduced session packages of five or ten sessions, but it's still easy to calculate your hourly rate and therefore very easy for your client to compare your hourly rate with someone else's. We need to find a way to get this comparison out of the way so that your prospect focuses on the immense value you offer, not the price. We will explore this issue in this book, too.

Back to our scenario, the client agrees to work with you and starts coming for their first sessions. You do a great job and the client gets better. After five or six sessions, the client is starting to feel quite good again.

This is the point where we run into problems. They start thinking that what has been done is probably good enough and the next week they "need" to visit family or they have a work trip coming up. All of a sudden, life starts getting in their way. You know, on the other hand, that they should come for another four or five sessions to resolve their issues once and for all.

But the client has not committed to that. They only committed to get their problem fixed. In the client's eyes, their issue is already sufficiently fixed. So, the client stops coming, has not had a transformational experience, and probably needs to come again. Will they come back to you? Who knows? Maybe they will try someone else who can "fix" them.

Now the client hasn't attained what they really wanted, you haven't achieved what you really wanted, and 40 percent of potential revenue has been left on the table. Now that is a loss-loss, not a win-win. Yes, there are positive outcomes here and you certainly can build a successful practice like that, but what do you truly value and what serves your vision? I wrote this book to show you a different way, a path that you can follow to make a bigger impact, perhaps a global impact, all while building a business that is scalable and moves you toward geographical, financial, and time freedom.

Even if your program has few participants, it's still worth doing it because simply getting someone to commit to go all the way creates a win-win for all parties involved. On top of that, you'll be walking the path to a more abundant life for yourself, your family, and your clients.

For this exact reason, we decided to create a transformational experience for our clients. Now we have a program that maps out the complete pathway from stress and pressure to time- and money-freedom as an influential wellness entrepreneur.

Give yourself the "green light" and start moving faster than self-doubt. Move away from having to sell yourself and instead sell a transformational journey that empowers your clients and doesn't try to fix them.

Remember what we talked about earlier in this book. You can't fix anyone. All you can do is focus on changing yourself and sharing your experience and knowledge confidently so that you can make a real impact across all aspects of life. If you want to move faster than self-doubt, dedicate one hour every morning to working on your business and the activities that are most important to achieving your vision.

The worst thing that happens to all of us is that we first try to get small tasks out of the way. For example, you do your emails and social media first or you treat your clients; only then you work on your program. If we don't stay focused, we risk getting caught up in the hustle and bustle of life; then, at the end of the day, our energy and productivity are low. At this point, we either do very little or nothing at all to work on our growth and dreams.

Let's turn it around, like we did with our business. Instead of offering a website with online marketing training, we started to only offer online marketing training and threw in a website for free. Do the same with your day. Start each day by working on your growth and dreams and throw the busy work in for free.

9

THE MONEY MINDSET

"Money and success don't change people;
they merely amplify what is already there."

—Will Smith

TIME TO TALK ABOUT MONEY. One of the most important concepts I teach and repeat all the time is our Wellness Product Ecosystem™. It's a framework to develop different products and assets for your business that take your clients and customers on a journey. We will talk about this concept in detail and how you can implement it in your business in the second half of this book. A crucial aspect of this model is that you have low-level entry products and at least one highly profitable product. There have been many occasions where I have held a workshop or had a one-on-one conversation with a wellness business owner where I outlined how you can create enough exposure to sell a scalable program online and make a global impact using this model. When it comes to implementing it, one of the biggest hurdles is pricing the highly profitable product. There is a general hesitancy with small business owners, especially in the health and wellness industry, to charge a highly profitable amount for their services. This causes them to undervalue themselves and get stuck in a small game that is frustrating and often taxing. As a business owner, you need to focus on selling this highly profitable product because once you sell it consistently, your whole business and life will change. Let me explain.

As soon as you have a system in place to build and educate an audience of the right people (those who align with you), you create a client journey that is valuable and helpful every step of the way. As someone progresses on that journey, they invest more time and money to better understand your world. Some people will drop off at the beginning, some will progress a bit further, and only a few will make it all the way. Clients who fully align with your ideal client profile will fully commit and be willing to pay what you and your service are truly worth. Because of the journey they have been on, these people understand that the life transformation you provide cannot be measured by price. However, every person who embarked on that journey received value. In one way or another, you assisted them on their journey. That's how you truly have an impact on the world. We help people not one-by-one, but by using a combination of one-to-one work, group work, videos, online courses, blogs, speaking, and so forth. Later we'll examine this combination further, but its core is that it takes affluent prices to create this type of impact.

Somewhere down the track of building our business, hustling and creating, we start to lose a bit of perspective. When you think about how you can change your business for the better so you can live a freer and happier life, you come to the point where you have to charge more money, not for the sake of earning more money, but to create an upward empowering spiral that enables you to share more and leverage your value so you can help more people.

Even so, many people hesitate to increase the price. My business life has also been filled with this type of talk. There are some concepts, ideas, and general wisdom you need to hear over and over again until someone explains it the way you need to hear it in the right context and when you are at the right place. In this chapter, I will share my version of money mindset in the hopes that you are in the right place after reading the previous chapters and that I have the words to create a new paradigm for how you charge for your products and services.

Money is generally associated with negativity, particularly among holistic practitioners and wellness business owners. Isn't it great if you could offer your services for free so everyone could take advantage of them? You're right. Despite growing up in a loving environment, money was always the devil. People with money were arrogant, and one didn't talk about money. My grandfather used to say, "One doesn't talk about money, one simply has it."

The money mindset still affects me today and may never leave me when it comes to my family. One time, my mother called me upset and worried about charges on her credit card that she didn't recognize. After she contacted her bank, she was told that the charges related to a video streaming service. Then she called me, not knowing what that meant. In a matter of seconds, my heart began to race and I felt a sense of stress and anxiety in my chest. I went into flight mode. My mother's call about charges on her credit card and the potential of me being the reason for that made me feel like the world was ending. Upon communicating with the company, they refunded her credit card and apologized for their error.

Throughout my life, there have been many times when I wasn't honest about money or didn't take responsibility for my financial choices for a long time, a situation that adversely affected my parents financially. I'm not proud of that, to say the least. In the case of money, I remember the mistakes I made as a child, and my subconscious remembers that advice. Money is hard to come by and it is a very stressful matter. People are bombarded with news stories every night about how unsecure the internet is and how all payments made online can potentially lead to fraud.

The point is that even though I have my money under control now, those subconscious beliefs remain and can still cause me to go off course when certain triggers come up. In business, those core beliefs can be so deeply ingrained that they can stay with you for eternity, and if you don't learn to recognize your triggers, you won't be able to respond to them, which will always block your progress. There will be a glass ceiling for you that you will never be able to break, and unless you become aware of this problem and address it, you will never have the impact on your business that you want.

As well as our internal issues about money, there is also the external issue of how big companies are exploiting our world. We could probably write innumerable tomes about the destruction of our environment and the greed of big corporations. Media sensationalizes all of this, and we have a beautiful stew of "Money stinks and whoever has money is a bad person."

From this perspective, charging highly profitable prices is often associated with appearing like "them" and no one wants their friends and family to assume they follow that example. However, charging for the true value of your service and the positive impact on the environment and your communities justifies the profits that are essential to abundance. Without abundance, there is no real impact or change. After you are overcome with fear and self-doubt, you have to start building a client experience and a highly profitable product.

Our attitude toward money is influenced by our childhood experiences as well as the world we see today. The fear engendered by such thoughts prevents us from charging more for excellent services, thereby driving our prices down. Subconsciously, we are not giving ourselves the go-ahead. Those childhood beliefs and what the media tells us cause us to stay in our ruts, keep us out of the spotlight, and make us stay small.

What does that mean for how I talk to potential clients? How confident am I in sales conversations, my investments, and the way I present myself? What about my dreams? What can I do to be a wellness advocate and take advantage of capitalism? These thoughts often cross my mind, and I develop new answers constantly.

We need to break this cycle because the world requires people like you. Millions of people are in need of health and well-being solutions due to the actions of less aware people in power and the social and environmental damage they have caused.

Keeping yourself in an invisible cage because you don't want to play the game won't change anything. By playing the game and playing well, we can make the world a sustainable, harmonious, and abundant place for everyone. Taking care of yourself first is the only way to be able to give something away for free.

Consider this: money is a tool. If you struggle with your money mindset and believe that there isn't enough money in the world, or that you shouldn't charge more for your services, or whatever the roadblock may be for you, remember that money is a tool. It's neither good nor bad. It's a form of energy that's used for good and for bad, or not at all. The force of a hammer can hit a nail and hang up a family portrait or result in a painful thumb injury. It can also just sit in the shed doing nothing. It's all about how you use the hammer.

That part is usually easy to understand. The real challenge is to absorb this and then make the development of that skill a priority. As soon as you begin, you will discover all those internal roadblocks. How much money can I charge? How will others perceive me? And so on. This is why I talked about first overcoming your fears, self-love, self-responsibility, and life whispers. It is important that you pull together all those principles and remind yourself of the deep inner calling you have to break that glass ceiling and push yourself out of the cage. The following is a lesson I learned from a great sales professional named Petar Lackovic to figure out how much you are worth in dollars. His advice was to increase your prices by 20 to 30 percent until more than 3 out of 5 potential clients say no. It was his philosophy that if you sold more than three out of five prospects, you were undervaluing yourself.

In 2016, I charged $80 per hour for consulting sessions. As a result of hearing Petar speak about increasing prices, I made it a part of my training to increase my hourly rate by 20 to 30 percent every time I signed up a new client. I increased my rate every single time by $20 to $30 until I am now at $250 an hour.

Think about that for a moment. Have you ever felt badly if one person said they couldn't afford your service or product? What would your business look like if you raised your prices until more than three out of five people said no? You must keep pushing up prices until you get 3 No's from 5 people. Only then will you know how much is possible.

Taking a look at the numbers, you can see how freeing this is. Let's say that you charge $100 per hour and sell five out of five prospects. That's $500 in total for five one-hour sessions. Let's say you increase your price by $30 and sell four out of five units. That's a total of $520, but for only four hours of work instead of five. Let's say you do another $30 per hour so you get to $160 per hour and you sell three out of five. That's a total of $480 but for only three hours instead of five. What could you do with those additional two hours? Get more business at this new highly profitable price? Spend more time with the family? Does pro bono work for those who really need it? Imagine the possibilities. Obviously, this is a fictive ideal situation, but you can read the principle between the lines. The idea is to find your true value unhindered by what others do, social norms, or your own internal roadblocks. Don't be afraid of upsetting a client, being rejected or being judged by others. Step into your power and embrace that the additional time and money that will flow to you will be used for good. It also doesn't mean you can't help those who can't pay your top prices. This is about what you put out there officially and then figuring out how you can help people in need.

When I began my career in hospitality, one of the first things I learned was that people pay different prices at different times depending on a variety of factors. This practice, which was invented by the big airlines, is known as revenue management. It is almost impossible for someone sitting next to you on a plane or staying in a hotel room across the hall to pay exactly the same price as you did, even if they bought the same thing. They may have booked a year earlier than you, or booked through a referral system or before a particular event had been announced. This is absolutely normal in those industries and everyone accepts it. We charge different prices for the same services, so why not differentiate by skill level, confidence level, or business journey? You must recognize your true value and stand up for it!

Think about how you can use this in your business. Can you offer early bird tickets for booking three to six months in advance? Could weekends be more expensive than weekdays to fill less busy periods? Is it possible to book an emergency session for a higher price? Modeling things after highly effective methods from other industries and locations can do much. Keep an eye out!

You should never live for money. That is clear to me, and I believe it is to you as well, but what if you needed the resources to make the change, to make the impact you are seeking, to fulfill your life's purpose? It is part of your life's purpose to help as many people as possible. This book is intended to help you live a life of fulfillment, fun, flow and freedom while making a global impact. A friend of mine once described making money is like drinking water. You need to drink water every day to live but drinking water is not your life's purpose. However, we all need to drink water to achieve optimal health, right?

It is the same with money. We need to make money consistently and manage it well to achieve our dreams and purpose in life unless, of course, you are on a purely spiritual pathway and want to become a monk. Since you are reading this book, that tells me otherwise. The purpose of this book is to help you get into the flow of your wellness business, not to help you hide in a remote corner. I am not saying there is no value in becoming a monk, I am just saying it is not the best route for everybody.

By shifting how you view money and establishing new core beliefs about wealth and prosperity, you come to realize whether money is good or bad . I believe that in the hands of people like you, it will be good. If I can help you to earn a million dollars from this book in the next three years, you will use as much of that sum as possible to make the world a better place and ultimately reduce suffering in the world.

That is what counts!

When you decide deep down that money in your hands will enable you to activate your potential and move the world toward wellness and less suffering, you empower yourself to overcome your fears, self-doubt, and play a bigger game.

10

THE END OF THE INNER GAME

"Whether you think you can or you can't, you're right."

—Henry Ford

THE INNER GAME I play constantly to improve, adapt, and fulfill my life purpose is what actually makes life worth living for me. Relationships I build with business people as well as with my family are exceptional. This is possible if done the right way, out of love and kindness, not out of greed. Grow as a person on the inside and you will be able to empathize more with family, build a sustainable business on all levels, and have more choices to do what you love.

I hope that you now feel a fire in your belly and a sense of YES, I CAN DO THIS. Before we dive into the second part of this book and what you actually can do to avoid the slump after the high, I want you to take some action right now. There is all the excitement and hype after a "Can Do" speech, but when you get home, everything plummets into a deeper pit because you realize you have no idea what to do. My personal rituals include daily meditation and exercise before starting the day. The combination of a strong mind and body will allow you to fully experience your day and take on any challenge that arises. For your

Inner Game, it is most important that you work on yourself every day. Take the time to work on your business and toward your true potential, just as you do for client bookings.

The most challenging but also most rewarding game you can play in life is the one that lies within. Your Inner Game and personal growth are like the roots of a tree that grow beneath the surface, hidden from view no matter where you are in your business journey. If you want to grow on the outside, your inner strength must grow at the same time and pace. In fact, the more you nurture your roots, the faster you will grow with your business.

Keep in mind that it is essential to bounce back and forth between inner and outer, always taking another step on each side. Step-after-step helps you get one little step further by influencing the other side. If you want to be fulfilled and happy, you can't focus on just one side. It is important to progress both in the Inner and Outer Game to have a purpose-driven business that creates positive change and brings you fulfillment.

Throughout the pages to follow, I will discuss the Outer Game and outline the actions you need to take and break down the steps you need to take so they are explained as simply as possible. Are you ready? Here we go.

PART III

The Outer Game

1

PRODUCTS, SERVICES, AND PRE-SOLD CUSTOMERS

"Products don't sell, product ecosystems do."

—Daniel Priestley

BEFORE WE GO INTO STRATEGIES and concepts around growing and systemizing your business, we need to define and explain some terms that we will use differently from now on.

Firstly, we need to clarify what we mean by "product" and what we mean by "service". We'll start with "product".

In order to move away from the session-by-session approach, selling time for money, everything that you offer in your business needs to be packaged up and presented like a product. Productizing your services allows you to sell features and benefits that are a complete solution to a client's problem.

Selling your time for money will always feel awkward to most people. This is totally normal because it feels like you're selling yourself. If I think about the wording "selling myself" alone, it makes me feel uncomfortable. Unless you have been given exceptional confidence and self-belief, this setup will always be a hard sell that just doesn't feel right.

Most people avoid selling because they hate it, mainly because it feels like you have to sell yourself.

You aren't required to sell if you're part of a wellness or similar clinic because the clinic handles all marketing, prospecting, and follow-up. You can hide behind the clinic's facade so you don't have to deal with these issues. However, you are also completely dependent on the clinic, and it is likely you will not be able to break through that glass ceiling. Your job is pretty decent, and you have some tax benefits since you are self-employed. This isn't a bad thing at all, but it also keeps you where you are.

Since there are 24 hours in a day, and if you also have family commitments and your own well-being to consider, you will only have a limited amount of time each day to work on your business. You can only scale time and sales by increasing your prices. This was demonstrated in an earlier chapter of the book. Some clinics may not even allow you to increase your prices, since there are already five other practitioners helping their clients with the same problems as you do who are already charging less. Your office will feel empty very quickly if you try to work in those conditions. However, even if you can increase your prices without losing too many clients, you need to remember that you want to help more people, not fewer. With premium prices, you can only treat those who can afford it.

Let's consider a product such as a book. What would you do? What would it be like to sell the book? I think you would begin your description by explaining how the book empowers someone to make changes in certain areas of their life. Possibly you could explain what it does not do and who it works best for. Then you talk about how easy it is to use the book and what else you can do with it. Do you see how none of this is about you? You're not the one doing the job; it's the product. You are a guide, helping someone to make a decision about whether what's in front of them would suit them. You are not selling yourself anymore.

You can achieve the same result with your "services". Develop an end-to-end solution for your ideal client, describing the benefits, the features, and how all of that will benefit their lives. You then set a price based on the value of those features and benefits, and voilà, you have a product.

While I know this approach may not be easy initially, I hope you see the point of creating a product and packaging your services so that you don't have to sell yourself.

Another huge benefit of having a product is that prospects will be more inclined to commit to the whole solution at a time when they feel the most pain and feel the most energetic. In other words, you do not leave about 40 percent of the money on the table because your client stops coming halfway through, as we discussed in the beginning of the book.

In order to grow your business successfully, you must remove yourself from the equation because you are often standing in your own way. You can achieve this by productizing your services. I will show you how to create a whole Wellness Product Ecosystem™, complete with features, benefits, and clear logistics on how to deliver it, which will completely transform the way you approach selling and will transform your business.

You will have more casual, personal sales conversations. During these conversations, you will feel confident and relaxed and may even find joy in them. With a proven system packaged into a product, you can enjoy the conversation without having to put yourself on the line.

Providing a complete solution to a client will also greatly increase their results since they committed themselves to doing it all and not stopping halfway through. When a product is a complete solution, it will lead to true transformations. Once you understand the process and get it right, you can automate it and even teach it to others.

In the next few pages, we will talk a lot about products, so remember what I mean by that and how packaging your services helps you on many levels on your journey to becoming an influential wellness entrepreneur.

Having learned what a product is, we can now see why it is important to create products for your business instead of selling your time for money. So, what about service? Every business in the world should have products and services. Is it possible to have both? Well, it just depends on what you mean when you say products or services. You just learned that any business can and should have products. You need services to market, sell, and deliver those products. It's the cherry on top!

If someone comes to your sessions or asks you questions on your social media, how do you interact with them? Are you friendly? Do you try to solve their problems right away? How do you follow up, making sure their problem is solved? Ultimately, your whole network, your entire business model, is your service. The better your service, your marketing and sales, the better your customer retention will be.

In my experience, small business owners tend to make a common mistake when they start their first venture into the world of online marketing. As soon as you put yourself out there in the online world, you become vulnerable, and people are bolder online since they can hide behind a screen. Consequently, we never stop getting negative reviews and complaints, and you may feel anger, frustration, and resentment.

In these situations, what often happens is that the business owner reacts rather than responds and leaves an unhelpful comment. Has this ever happened to you? Maybe you have written one of those knee jerk comments and regretted it later. We discussed how your business is your baby. Your feelings are understandable. You will, however, be associated with your name and reputation as a business entity. If you do that on a platform you don't control, such as Facebook or Google, you will have a very difficult time removing it. The process of removing a negative response from an online client can typically take weeks or months. Anything can stay online indefinitely. That's great when you're creating content in the right place, but disastrous when it comes from the wrong place. When it comes to your online marketing, a single negative comment will almost overshadow a hundred positive ones. Therefore, watch what you say.

In fact, a bad comment can help you offer better services and grow your business. I learned a lot about that in the hospitality industry. You won't believe how many obscure and absolutely ridiculous complaints and journeys there are. Things like "the carpet in my room and the couch are half a meter further to the right than they appear on the picture online," and that isn't a joke. At the Four Seasons in Sydney, I had a similar complaint while working at the front desk. We trained receptionists to make the guests happy no matter what, because not only do we want happy returning guests, we can create an even more satisfied guest if they make a complaint. Hospitality professionals call this the "Complaint Paradox". I will explain. If a customer complains about their meal or hotel room, it could be a bad or a very good thing. The difference is how you handle that complaint. You can lose business if you react poorly or ignore the complaint, or you can, on the other hand, create an experience for the guest that will blow him/her away with great service. This is something of which all five-star hotels are aware. By being kind and understanding and making sure the complaint gets resolved, you can create a more loyal customer than you would have had without the complaint. What a paradox, right?

Every customer complaint has to follow a certain sequence. Ensure you fully understand your customers; then, offer a solution and something that makes the customer happy. They could get a free item or a discount the next time they come back. As they wait for the issue to be resolved, such as being refunded or having their room ready, you need to communicate consistently with them, to ensure they know you haven't forgotten about them. Once the issue is resolved, you follow up with them later to make sure everything is to their satisfaction.

Now, that's five-star service. A great service not only resolves an issue but goes above and beyond what is expected. This can transform a simple complaint into an exceptional experience that would not have been possible without the complaint.

The service you provide is your concern for each client and for those who might become clients. It has to do with how you treat others. No matter what is thrown at you in business, do it with a smile and real care. Whenever you receive a complaint, take a deep breath, put it into perspective, and remember the complaint paradox. You can use every complaint as an opportunity to show how exceptional your company is.

Here's another piece of advice for delivering outstanding service: Say your clients' names at least three times when you first meet them. Knowing clients' names makes them feel special. Many people to whom I give this advice say they feel awkward when they do this, but let me assure you that it has a wonderful effect on others. People love hearing their names and there is nothing awkward about it. I was first made aware of the fact that people love to hear their own names when I read Dale Carnegie's *How to Win Friends and Influence People*. As a result, I also tried to pay attention to how I felt when I heard my name. I highly recommend that you give it a try. After a while, it will feel normal to you. There is a certain pride and joy that comes with names. They have a lot of power. Saying a person's name at least three times on check-in was a very important rule at the Four Seasons Sydney and I started to learn dozens of names every day when working there. I remember telling myself that I have a terrible time with names. There are so many people who say that. If you say someone's name three times the first time you meet, I guarantee that you will remember their name the next time you meet.

A business should offer exceptional products and services. In the following pages, we will explore how to accomplish that consistently and in a way that does not consume all of your free time. It is great to offer five-star service, but if you spend hours every week taking care of everyone individually, you will soon run out of gas.

We need to understand one last term, pre-sold customers. Our sales conversation conversion rate is somewhere above 80 percent. We are successful not because we are exceptional salespeople, but because we talk to the right people. We only talk to "pre-sold" customers.

At the beginning of my business, I remember trying to make one sale at a time, going to networking events and meeting people in person. This traditional method involves making an initial connection with someone and then following up. You can be lucky if that person has a problem that is big enough to make them take action and agree to meet.

To meet people, I had to drive between thirty minutes and an hour one way. Maybe you meet that person another two or three times before you reach the point where you talk about signing up for one of your offers. Often, the job is small, a single session or two, and you spend all that time trying to close the sale. Because I love networking, I meet a lot of people and make connections quickly. I really enjoy it because it's my nature. After hearing my pitch and learning about my work for ten minutes, I once met an NLP practitioner who seemed intrigued. Immediately following the networking event, we grabbed a coffee. It was difficult for me to communicate my true value to him in a clear and efficient manner because I didn't have a sales process in place. So, we talked for 45 minutes over coffee and decided to meet again to "discuss things further". My second attempt to schedule a coffee catch-up – about a week later – was successful. I drove thirty minutes to the café, talked for another hour, and then drove back again without achieving a sale. As a result, I followed up again and after another week we had a third one-hour conversation at the same café before I finally proposed: "Would you like to book this six-month program at a $5,000 upfront fee?" He responded that he wasn't ready to invest yet, because he had just started the business. It took until the third meeting for me to establish this because I was desperate for a sale and too afraid to get to the point. Let's look at how much time I spent to establish that he wasn't interested! We had three meetings and each drive to meet this potential client took about an hour. The first "coffee catch-up" took 45 minutes and the second and third about an hour each. That's almost six hours already! In addition, I had to remember to follow up after the meetings and to lock in the next steps. That's probably another forty minutes. We are now at an amazing six hours and forty minutes to find out that the person was not ready to work with me, which could have been accomplished in about 15 minutes, as you will learn later in this book. Does this scenario sound familiar to you?

No matter how you look at it, this method will sooner or later leave you frustrated and exhausted. You are not only hurting your own business, but also hurting the other person by wasting both your own time and theirs.

I personally don't do coffee catch-ups anymore when it comes to sales. That doesn't mean I don't meet people for coffee in person. If I see real value in it, I quite enjoy that. The sales process, however, must be structured and crystal clear, so it can be a valuable part of your business. Chatting in person can have other benefits, making it time well spent if, for example, you want to create a strategic business partnership. This will be discussed later in the book when we look at how partnerships can help you grow your business faster. Valuing your time is important not only for your Outer Game, but also for you to grow as a person. It all comes down to your Inner Game of overcoming your fears and taking responsibility for your inner blocks, so you can position yourself as an expert and become the person you require for the future you envision.

We need two things in place to make this work: a sales process that is effective and a marketing system that generates "pre-sold" customers. Later, we will discuss the sales process. Now, let's focus on the term "pre-sold" customers.

Pre-sold customers are those who have already seen your content so that they understand your value and why working with you is right for them. Perhaps they watched a video, read an article, or saw something you posted on social media. Pre-sold customers have educated themselves about you and what you do and aligned themselves not only with your services, but also with your values and the story behind what you do.

People have different theories about how much and how often they need to consume content about you and your business in order to buy from you. A study posted on Conductor, a website that empowers entrepreneurs and innovators, demonstrated that "consumers are 131 percent more likely to buy from a brand immediately after consuming early-stage, educational content." This means you have to first create educational content to build knowledge, familiarity and trust with your audience. This will make it much easier to sell or make sure you create pre-sold customers.

Many studies have tried to analyze how much content needs to be consumed on average to build enough trust. Some studies claim it's about eleven pieces of content, others say it's nine to ten hours spent consuming content.

The fact is, if you want to become a better salesperson, you need to share and leverage your knowledge. Few people in the world like sales, although a few do. That's hard to believe, right? Personally, I have a love-hate relationship with sales. It's a lot of fun when there are clear processes in place and everything goes smoothly. When there is a piece missing or I can see from the beginning that I do not want to work with this person, it is not fun because I have to gather my courage, trust my intuition, and turn the prospect down quickly. By concentrating on creating pre-sold customers, the latter situation is less likely to occur. The strategy outlined later in this book makes it almost impossible.

To make your sales more enjoyable, educate your audience to a point where it fully understands what you do, how you do it, and why you do it. As a result, you will create pre-sold clients, and the better you create these types of prospects, the less painful your sales conversations will be, and the less effort you will have to put into converting prospects into customers.

Your wellness business will shift from chasing the sale to attracting your ideal clients. People will naturally select and deselect themselves as you share your story and knowledge. People are more likely to get off the fence if you include more of your personality. Before you talk to someone, you want them to decide whether they want to work with you. You can still connect with people without actually being with them. Online, they will continue to explore your offer until they say yes, I want to talk, or no, I don't.

The best way to educate and build "know, like, and trust" is to give away knowledge and helpful practices. The more you do that, the better. But you have to do it strategically with the right language so it is a win-win. Your audience wins, and you and your business wins.

People express concern that giving away their intellectual property for free is harmful to their business, which is a very common misconception that comes from fear and the feeling that everything is a competition. Today, everyone carries the knowledge of the world in their pocket (or handbag). In other words, if I want to learn about what you do or anything else, I can simply Google it. No matter what I want to make, whether it's a cupcake for dessert or a rocket to fly to the moon, I can find instructions on the internet.

One thing that can't be done by Google (or other search engines), however, is to provide the human element, which is more intangible. Only the human element can provide the exact order of stepping stones and the accountability that suits your unique situation. It wouldn't matter if you provided all your knowledge for free in the form of PDF reports, articles, videos or any other form of content. In the end, people will need you to achieve their goals because they can't put the puzzle pieces together on their own and they will probably fall off track without your accountability. How often have you downloaded a free PDF guide, online course or other material and not achieved what you were looking for, although you had all the information?

Yes, there are some rare individuals that are so dedicated they will eventually succeed, but they will do that regardless of how generously you share your knowledge, or not. But imagine what they would say to their peers and especially online if they were able to access all they require through *your* website or other channels like YouTube or social media. They would become your best advocates and walking billboards for your business. Imagine the impact if you showcased a case study of someone who achieved their goals themselves using your free content, and how many people would contact you as a result.

Once people discover your modality, feature program or course with your free content, they will realize they need your support and guidance! They will go where they received the free information in the first place. This is how it works. You need more sales to grow your business, and to make more sales, you need to help more people for free.

Isn't that beautiful? When you focus on sharing value and building your audience, you become known for something and have a greater impact on the world.

So now that we understand what we mean by product, service and pre-sold customers, let's dive in and build that lifestyle business you dream of.

2

THE WELLNESS PRODUCT ECOSYSTEM™

ONE OF MY BASIC RULES to grow and build any business is to mimic and adapt what the big guys do. This means observing how successful companies operate, and then applying those concepts and strategies in my own business in my own way.

No matter what we think from an ethical point of view about some of these large companies, there is a reason why they have been able to build to such heights.

For example, I am a big fan of Apple products. I almost never buy anything else as their devices are seamless and intuitive. They sync with each other. When I work on my phone, I know that I can access my notes, calendar entries, text replacements, and all other stuff on my laptop and iPad instantly. It saves me a lot of time and headaches. Moreover, I really love the look and feel of their products. It's like being a part of a whole system of interlinked products that make my life easier. That's hugely powerful.

Ten years ago, Apple released the first iPhone, and a short time later, Samsung released its first smartphone and the two had to compete. Samsung spent around 14 million dollars advertising its smartphone.

Apple instead advertised its iPod for half of Samsung's budget. The deal? They offered a free product when you bought an iPod, which enticed the customer to buy the iPhone. That free product was iTunes.

Apple discovered that having all your music on you at all times was something everyone wanted. So people who bought an iPod with iTunes, including playlists and songs, would naturally buy the iPhone as well. It's much easier to promote a $100 product like an iPod than a $1,000 product like a smartphone. Apple's return on investment in their advertising was through the roof compared to other smartphone companies like Samsung. Their most successful strategy was a free product to have all your music with you wherever you were, and this naturally led into other more profitable products like phones, laptops, and computers. In fact, their most profitable product is Apple Care. The Apple Care program lets you replace and repair your device over a period of two to three years, guaranteeing you a remarkable product experience. It's an "After Sale" product that requires very little input to create great value for the customer at a highly profitable price. To this day, Apple has a whole system of interlinked products that complement each other. It is only logical to move on to using another Apple product after the first. Apple's early success was built on this product ecosystem. Over the years, marketing changed a bit for Apple as it grew into one of the most successful companies in the world. In the beginning, though, this strategy allowed Apple to focus on the easy-to-sell products with their marketing and advertising. To become what Apple is today, Apple didn't sell devices. Apple sold and still sells a complete product ecosystem.

I thought about how I could apply this not only to my business but to my clients' businesses as well. That's when I developed the Wellness Product Ecosystem™. The model will offer you a way to build an ecosystem of products and assets for your business, just like Apple, so that you can market your own easy-to-sell product that leads into a highly profitable "Feature Product".

The Wellness Product Ecosystem™ (WPE) has four products:

1. The Freebie (e.g., iTunes)
2. The Entry Product (e.g., iPod)
3. The Feature Product (e.g., iPhone/Laptop)
4. The After Sale (e.g., AppleCare)

They all relate to each other and educate your audience, and they give your audience a better sense of how you do things. Then, they can begin to trust you. The first two products, the Freebie and the Entry Product, can help prospects gain a deeper understanding of what you offer. They can build "know, like, and trust" without you having to focus on your high-ticket Feature Product. Like with Apple, the last two products, the Feature Product and the After Sale, will be sold because people bought the first two.

It's imperative that each step in your WPE is of value and a win for the consumer. You can look at these four basic products as the major stepping stones for your clients' wellness journey. By creating products instead of services for your business, you put assets in place that you can leverage and automate. This is how large companies scale their businesses. Products have features, logistics, and a defined scope with a profit margin, all of which can be systematized and outsourced.

By identifying the stepping stones of each process, you can find specific software to do the job or find someone who is an expert in this area and get yourself out of the way for the jobs you don't want to do. This is absolutely crucial for your business's long-term success. We need to analyze the business processes we repeat again and again and identify ways to automate, systematize, and streamline the different aspects of the business. It's about efficiency.

Having grown up in Germany, I know a lot about efficiency! Everything is done to the greatest efficiency. One of my favorite pastimes with my dad and grandpa was making firewood so that we would have enough wood for the winter. Every summer, our tractor and trailer would take us down a dirt road to our beautiful little pine tree forest about thirty minutes away. Dead trees would be picked up and cut down, and then we would plan how to cut the branches and trunks into smaller pieces for the trailer.

Sounds simple enough, but I believe the method we used was like a mini-symphony of efficiency. The timing of our tasks would be perfect for each of us. While my grandpa felled the tree with my dad, I chopped the branches and marked the trunk for cutting. Once one tree was down, my grandpa would look for the next to cut, establishing exactly how the tree would fall so it would be easy to transport and process. During that time, my dad helped me cut the tree trunk to length. Then my dad would go back to my grandpa to fell the next tree, and I had to load up the trailer in time to chop off the branches from the newly fallen tree and repeat the process. There was constant adjusting and helping each other to make the process faster and more efficient. We would tease each other and push each other to get even more efficient, and the better we got, the more fun we had. I consider progress and efficient work to be hugely satisfying.

I remember my grandpa taking the lead (of course!) and constantly yelling, "We're slowing down!" In other words, one of us wasn't going fast enough (in his opinion) to keep the process moving so that nobody needed to wait. Efficiency was nonnegotiable. It was the same with chopping the wood for storage, building a fence, doing repairs, and shoveling snow in winter. Absolutely everything was done to perfection and we loved it.

Do you still wonder why Germany is known for efficiency and perfection? This was the norm for every household. In fact, when families or friends came together for a community project, those that didn't have the same mindset were quickly given a job where they wouldn't affect others.

Each of us has 24 hours in a day and, besides work, we must sleep, have fun with friends, and take care of our families. I urge you to be methodical and efficient when implementing the WPE, since it can quickly get overwhelming. As discussed early in this book, this really comes down to creating space. Time should be set aside for creating space as failing to do so will cause the work required to create your WPE to become overwhelming and a burden. That is the last thing I want for you. Make time to work on your business, rather than in your business.

Let's take a look at our WPE in more detail and see how you can implement this into your business and where you can automate processes.

The Wellness Product Ecosystem™ by Wellnesspreneur:

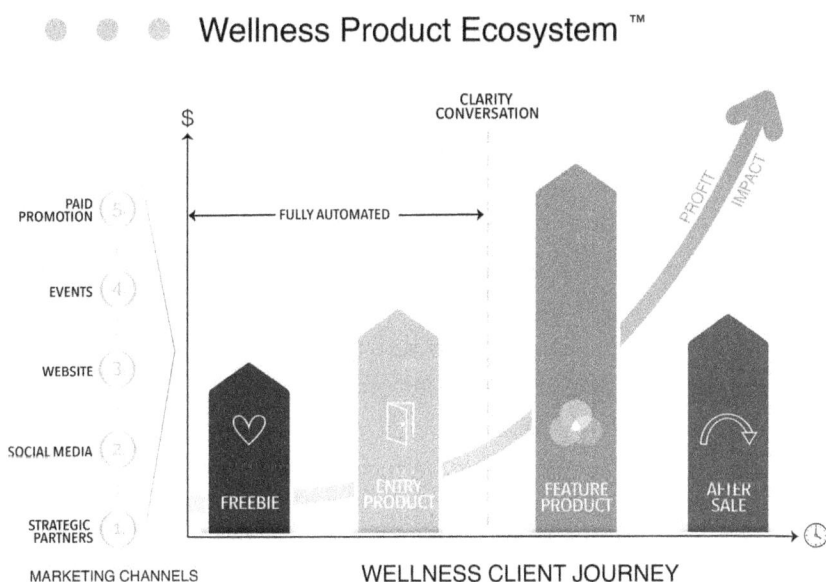

You can see the complete WPE above. On the very left are the five marketing channels in order of priority. All five channels lead into the first product, the Freebie, which then leads into the other products. You can see how all four products of the WPE relate to each other and to your marketing. Most wellness business owners make the mistake of spending thousands of dollars on a website, social media ads or promotional events without having clear products in place.

Look at how the Profit/Impact arrow flows from left to right. You can see that the first two products are not about making money but purely educating your audience and building "know, like and trust". The *real* power of online marketing is automating and leveraging the process of building an audience, nurturing that audience, and then booking calls with pre-sold customers. That's using your marketing to feed your Freebie and Entry Product sales, and then automating those stepping stones to get people to book in a call where you sell your Feature Product. Have a look at the WPE graph again and identify this process from the left to right of the WPE model above.

Now that you have a basic understanding of the model, let's look at the four products. The first two products on the left are the two that you need to build online, so you can automate them. The Freebie offers your audience a valuable quick win, usually in exchange for their name and email address with no charge, hence the name Freebie. It's a free first step for anyone who wants to learn more about what you do. The second step on the other hand, the Entry Product, can have a price that should be less than $500. For instance, you could offer a low-price online course to help your clients get started on their wellness journey. Your Entry Product could also be a significant investment of time only, instead of a financial commitment, such as a webinar or masterclass after your Freebie. The important part is that the Entry Product requires a higher commitment than the Freebie, whether time, money, or both. The Freebie and the Entry Product are designed to put people on a journey with you, one step at a time. I call this your "Wellness Client Journey".

The first two products lead into a "Clarity Conversation". After people experience your Freebie and Entry Product, you create clarity for your prospect about whether your Feature Product is right for them.

The Feature Product is your high-ticket and highly profitable offering. It needs to be a minimum of $1,000, ideally over $3,000. Think about a complete solution to your clients' problems. Pack everything into the Feature Product that will create a transformative experience for your clients, from what they are struggling with to feeling awesome. Make a list, get clear on how you deliver everything on that list, and then price it accordingly with a sufficient margin that will appropriately reward you for the exceptional value you are providing. Overcome your doubts, your fears, and your potentially limiting money mindset as we talked about in the first half of the book, and build your Feature Product without limitations. The WPE will do the selling!

The After-Sale is a logical next step after people experience your Feature Product. It could be a four-day retreat or a subscription to a mastermind group. Choose what you would enjoy the most but remember to set the price in a way that will create financial freedom for you. The people that reach this step love you. They have experienced several products on their Wellness Client Journey with you from your marketing channels all the way to the After Sale. At this point, you can truly charge the value that you are worth because your customers fully understand it. There is no big process needed to sell this product. You simply put it in front of those who bought your Feature Product.

While you share your value authentically and with ease through your various channels, the system leads a person to your highly profitable Feature Product, whatever that may be. Through this system you can bring in your values and the reasons why you do what you do without having to worry about selling.

Those who are new to marketing make the mistake of focusing their efforts on advertising and marketing their Feature Product or services without building, educating, and nurturing an audience. Then they wonder why there is no return on their efforts. Often, they give up after a short while and say, "This online thing is not for me. My approach should be the same as it has always been." Meaning, they rely on word-of-mouth and chase one sale at a time, have no time for the things they truly enjoy, and no freedom to choose because they are hoping people will just show up and buy. It's your responsibility to do great work not only once you have a customer, but also before and after.

Imagine, for example, that your business established a small following online and a hundred people downloaded your Freebie. Of those people, ten will buy your Entry Product, and of those ten, four will schedule a Clarity Conversation with you. One or two of those Clarity Conversations will result in a sale of $1,000 each. Would that change your marketing, your advertising, social media, and everything else you do in your business? As soon as you establish your WPE in your business and recognize your conversion numbers, you know exactly where to focus your marketing channels and how many Freebie downloads you need to turn a profit.

This is the true power of the digital world. You can systematize and automate the whole process from the Freebie all the way to booking for the initial conversation with you. Then you can focus on providing value, contributing to others, and having fun with your business marketing.

Having this system in place eliminates the need to worry about sales, since people take their next step at their own pace as they explore what you do and how you can help them. There is no force, only care and a willingness to help.

Sometimes we look at marketing and sales as this evil, unenjoyable task we have to do to stay in business or grow. In reality, it's an extension of what you do already, just at a larger scale and with a greater impact.

> *"You will have the most success online if you recreate what you do offline."*
>
> —Sebastian Hilbert

During the rest of this book, I will explain to you how you can build your WPE and start using your marketing channels effectively.

3

MY (MARKETING) HERO:
JAMES BOND

I FOUND THAT USING the five different marketing channels (presented in the next chapter) in combination with the WPE you can get yourself in front of customers and predict your sales. However, this step still needs to come from your Why and your Inner Journey. You will see results quickly if you bring in what's close to your heart and purpose and if you are diligent about it. To use and create all of these systems, products, and terminologies confidently, always keep in mind that you have to start from within. Then you will have the congruence and energy to attract the people who make all the difference to your life and business. You should apply the same principles to what you communicate via different channels and products.

I mentioned earlier that sales messages bombard us every day. How many of the billboard signs, radio advertisements, shop posters, and the like can you recall from the past 24 hours? Two? One? None? It's probably true that for more than 90 percent of the people reading this book, it'll be "none". In addition, many people who adhere to alternative medicine make a strong effort to avoid being exposed to this type of advertising.

We need to find another path. A more elegant way. In order to demonstrate a better solution, let's talk about my childhood hero: James Bond. You might be rolling your eyes now, but let me explain. I have so much fun watching this rather unrealistic and perfect spy get "the girl" and drive that cool car.

Imagine someone like me watching a James Bond movie. The movie I'm watching on TV is providing me with entertainment value. James Bond is my favorite movie, so I stay for as long as I can to get that value, as long as the film continues.

Every twenty to thirty minutes, the movie and therefore its value is interrupted by an advertisement that screams "Buy from me" for five to ten minutes. This is known as interruption marketing. What do most people do when this interruption takes place? They turn off the volume and go get tea or a snack. Then they come back for the value.

Our basic response has been to tune out these messages. So, unless you have a huge budget to consistently run this kind of interruption marketing to eventually catch someone off guard, it's almost impossible to get a return on investment through this approach.

A different approach is to use a form of marketing called product placement. Using James Bond as an example, you will notice that he always wears an Omega watch and drives an Aston Martin. I have a favorite classic car, which you can now guess. It's a 1963 Aston Martin DB5. While I am not a great fan of Omega watches, the point is that these products are always present without interfering with the movie and making me associate them with my hero.

Marketing should achieve the same result. Create a system that places your products in front of your audience all the time without interrupting your valuable message.

This is the reason why we have the automated part of the WPE. Getting this right will help you put your products in front of your audience, while sharing your value and expertise through your various channels.

Sharing content and creating it becomes so much more enjoyable once the system is built. It can be exhilarating to know what to do and to be assured that the sales will come from leveraging your knowledge throughout the various channels.

"Clarity is power."

—Tony Robbins

Your goals will become more realistic if you have a baseline for the number of downloads required to make a sale. The number of leads you generate per channel can be checked, and more importantly, which channels should be improved to get enough Freebie downloads to hit your goal.

When it comes to sharing value and product placement, we can't forget our agenda. In addition to sharing great content, we must also ask people directly to take the next step. We are usually very good at sharing value, educating others, and helping people wherever we can. All the people I work with say to me, "I just love to help people." It is important to ask others to do something and present our content in a way that makes people want more, something we generally do not do well. It is often feared that we come across as manipulative and salesy. We need to address this issue in order to effectively use any marketing channel.

Asking can take many forms. You can include a PS section in an email, a short "Call to Action" at the end of a video, or a simple paragraph at the end of a blog. If we fail to ask at the end, no matter how valuable the content is, we will quickly lose a lot of people. Your business will lose value from all the effort you put into creating content and sharing it with the world. However, it is also disappointing for those who are fascinated by what they have just consumed and then don't know how to proceed. Imagine yourself watching a great presentation like a TedTalk about a serious problem, and you feel that you really want to do something about it, but the presenter doesn't provide you with any next steps for taking action. Often, because it's hard to find the next step on your own, you will forget about the problem and move on to other things.

A great piece of content that raises an issue and asks questions creates an "open loop." The human brain is compelled to close open loops. This is something the TV industry knows very well and has used for years to keep you watching. How many times have you found yourself watching several episodes of a series on a streaming service when you only intended to watch one? The short two-minute scene at the end of the episode probably piqued your interest because you wanted to know what happens next. Even though each episode usually has its own closed content, there is always an underlying story that is used to keep you engaged. Watching a detective show like Sherlock Holmes is an example. A case is introduced at the start of the episode and Sherlock Holmes and his sidekick Watson try to solve it. At the end of every show, something shocking or significant happens in the plot. In the next episode, you might learn who Sherlock's archenemy, Moriarty, is or what the next case is. The outcome is unclear. The human brain needs to close this classic open loop.

Netflix is a master of using open loops. If you've ever binge-watched an entire series in one weekend, you know what I mean. It's just one more episode, right? Psychologists refer to this idea as the Zeigarnik Effect. In 1927, Bluma Zeigarnik, a Russian psychologist, was fascinated by the fact that waiters were able to remember several orders at a time over the course of a day. Zeigarnik observed that waiters remember orders only as long as they were "open". As soon as the order was completed, they forgot about it almost immediately.

I was a waiter for three years and I remember that quite well. In those days, if anyone had asked me about a completed order, I would have had trouble answering, but as long as an order was open, I knew who ordered what and when. It didn't matter if it took fifteen minutes for a coffee order or three hours for a seven-course dinner. As long as the order wasn't closed, I could keep the information in my short-term memory.

So, what does that have to do with open loops? Our minds keep spinning and thinking about things that are not completed. Orders at a restaurant, TV shows, or even running a two-day workshop or course all have the same effect. You can give your attendees a question to think about at the end of the day and they'll have thought hard about it by the next morning. The same goes for your marketing content. In your stories, try not to reveal exactly how things work, and instead introduce new information. Clearly state the questions and next steps that arise from what you just shared, but do remember to close the loop.

My great hero, James Bond, for instance, is gifted with gadgets like an exploding pen and a watch with an abseil rope. The gadgets are open loops that must be used. James Bond fans would feel cheated if the gadget wasn't used. James's use of the gadget in that crucial scene at the end of the movie makes me so happy. Not closing the loop leaves people feeling disappointed.

A great way to implement open loops in your business is to pick a specific step or part of your Feature Product and create a deep-dive seminar, workshop, or video series about it. At the beginning and the end of your seminar or course, you show your audience the complete path, meaning all the steps of your Feature Product and how it helps them to get from where they are to where they want to be. This will create an open loop, as they will get a part of your complete solution, but not all of it. With an open loop like this, you can give away as much as you want as long as you stay within that specific step or part of your Feature Product.

The Wellnesspreneur Growth Model that I use to demonstrate the value and process of my coaching program, for instance, has the Nine Wellness Growth Accelerators. I can give away as much as I want on any one, two, or three accelerators through an online training course, a two-day workshop, or even a one-week retreat. I begin and end my presentation by showing the complete model, my full solution to my audience's problems, and asking if anyone wants to explore the other accelerators. To me, this strategy is extremely powerful because it feels right. There is no deception. This is what we discussed, a genuine exchange of value, but an exchange with a purposeful business outcome to sustain us in our ability to keep sharing value and helping people.

When I first learned and implemented this open loop tactic, I was quite skeptical because of those old fears of manipulating people and not being honest. I then centered myself and I thought about why I do what I do. I realized it is important for me to use every tool and skill at my disposal to make the change I want to see in the world. At the end of the day, when someone chooses to work with me, they are getting ME. People will see my integrity, my genuine nature, and my willingness to help when they meet me. This is what counts, because I know that I have the right intentions and can deliver the results I promise.

Marketing and sales skills are indispensable if you want to build a thriving wellness business and make a global impact. You can wing it or outsource tasks you don't want to do, but when you don't understand what you outsource and ignore how people behave at a basic level for whatever reason, you are blindly hoping for the best. Hope is not a viable business strategy.

7

MARKETING CHANNELS

HAVING DISCUSSED THE TWO principles of product placement and open loops, we can now discuss each of the five marketing channels of the WPE, proceeding in the following order:

1. Strategic Partnerships
2. Social Media
3. Website
4. Events
5. Paid Promotion

It is important to follow the above order. As I explained earlier, advertising is the last channel for many reasons. Ads can really have a great impact on your business if all other marketing channels are working well for you. The power of advertising comes from leveraging what your business already knows works. Therefore, once you have built the system and used the other four channels to fuel it, you will have a working system that is worth taking to the next level through advertising.

Advertising alone, with just a product offering as the only component, is extremely difficult to make viable and expensive. It's different if you sell stationery, but you and I don't do that kind of business.

Alternatively, if you have a good social media presence and regularly get booked for other people's podcasts and speaking engagements, you can take advantage of advertising to promote what you already do and really market the potential of your business.

With your wellness business model established, you know how to create assets and products to attract your audiences and how to nurture them to a defined destination. The next step is to investigate the different channels in detail and see how we can make the most of them.

7.1 – Strategic Partners

In order to create massive exposure and grow your business, you need to find businesses that share your target market, offer complementary products, and align with your business vision and principles. Strategic Partnership is when you build and nurture relationships with such businesses so that you, they, and both of your customers benefit.

This gets me excited every time I think about it. It's totally understandable if you don't get excited. My partner in life and business, Teresa, always makes fun of me when we are discussing such strategic partnerships. I hope to pass some of that excitement on because once you grasp it, it is truly transformative.

Collaboration usually involves doing a workshop or referring clients to each other. It requires a great deal of trust and a strong relationship that has typically been built over months or even years. While this is the ultimate outcome of a partnership, it doesn't begin there. The question is where does it start from and how can we get there.

The first thing to remember is to start small. Find out who might be a suitable partner for you. Consider where your clients spend money elsewhere. Where do they go before they come to you and where do they go after they leave? Is there a cafe in the clinic where you work, or a place for lunch? Is there a gym or a health food store around the corner? What other healing practices complement your own? Those businesses are a good place to start.

After you identified five or more potential partner businesses, it is a matter of reaching out and asking if their owners would be interested in collaborating with you. The most incredible opportunities in your business will come from talking to others and building relationships. So, the more people you talk to, the better.

Ultimately, it is about finding the right business owners who have the right product. Unfortunately, business owners don't always have the right mindset, and those with the right mindset don't always have the right product and audience. Mindset and alignment with values and vision are key, however. Often the rest can be worked out from there.

You also want your strategic partners to really understand and value what you do. The information you give them needs to be clear, precise, and understandable. For example, how many people actually understand osteopathy, kinesiology, or life coaching? If your profession is too hard to understand, it will be difficult for your partner to make referrals to you.

Going back to the partner mindset and alignment, you can usually tell pretty early on whether someone will make a good partner. I remember talking with the owner of a web design firm who had a product which seemingly complemented mine. I asked him where he was in his life, and right away he talked about his business. Then I asked: "What do you do outside of business?" He couldn't answer the question, or didn't want to. It was important to me to find out if we shared the same values and maybe even saw the world from the same perspective. I knew if that was the case, collaborating and helping each other would be easy and a no-brainer. With this guy, however, I couldn't get past the business conversation and I knew this wasn't going anywhere. After I shared a short pitch about my business, he straight away told me how I could promote his website services and earn a commission. BAM! That was it. Our values were not aligned. How could I promote his services without any alignment on our vision and values? There was no way I would put my credibility on the line.

The other red flag was that all he was interested in talking about was selling *his* product and how great *he* was. When it comes to collaborating with others and running a business, it's not about you! You are embarking on a journey bigger than yourself when you tap into your life's purpose and true self. In the end, even if you take nothing else away from this book but that, I'd feel blessed that my time spent on it was worthwhile.

The people you meet and the connections you make will be incredible. Yes, you will have duds like the guy I spoke to. However, that was one out of a hundred. Conversations typically move in a different direction.

Once you ask someone what they do outside of business, you will find something you align with and the conversation becomes fun. You bring it to a personal level. Then you just enjoy making the connection and when you know that person is someone you like and want to get to know more, you ask them if there is anything you can do for them. If there is alignment in vision and values, everything flows.

It is possible for these 15- or 20-minute conversations to change one's life. Chat a bit and establish the connection, then set up the next step. To get something tangible out of each conversation, it is always helpful to have a few ideas about what you might do together. It takes time to build these partnerships.

One of the simplest ways to get started is to ask if you can do cross promotion by sharing each other's Freebies. The Freebie is the first step in your WPE and Wellness Client Journey. You do not risk your credibility too much by offering a free resource to another person since this is a completely value-based offer. You run a high risk of losing your credibility as an expert if you try to refer clients right away or start doing workshops without knowing how that person will effectively deliver.

Make sure your partner follows through first, and then you can move forward. This approach allows you to actively find people with whom to share your Freebie. I have a list of about thirty people I can contact and ask to share my Freebie. All of those thirty relationships started with a phone call to build trust and align our vision and values. Your Freebie can be shared with your partners multiple times as well. They will grow their audience continuously if they are growing their business. As you continue to collaborate and share free resources, you will continue to gain new leads and business. Partner relationships should always be win-win-win. It must be beneficial to the partner, the customer, and you. It is not enough to share a resource or offer from someone else without understanding how it benefits you. Your benefit should also not be a financial exchange such as a commission. By doing so, you will only be an affiliate in the eyes of the other person. Exchanges need to be of equal value, and both parties must aim for a long-term relationship.

If you partner up with local cafés, they could offer you vouchers for free coffee and you could supply them with a flyer offering your Freebie. You should make sure that this flyer is given to each customer with their coffee order or is on view at each table and at the coffee counter. A fair exchange must take place. Provide your clients with a coffee voucher so that they reciprocate. Don't just put your flyer next to the newspaper stand or, worse, next to the fifty other flyers they have lying around. That is why alignment and personal connection with these partners is crucial. You won't get this kind of deal if you just show up with your flyers one day and ask, "Hey, can I put these flyers out here?" Your Freebie or Entry Product should become part of their service offer and add value. To get there you need to nurture the relationship first and show them how this relationship would benefit them, their customers, and you.

These "standard" flyers are often found in clinics, offices, and cafés that showcase all the various services a business offers on the common trifold brochure. The text usually reads, "Look at all the awesome things we do. We offer Reiki, massage, acupuncture, and so much more! You can come in for a free consultation to see how awesome we are." Terrible move. First of all, it's not about you and, secondly, 99 percent of the people who pick up that flyer don't know you, don't like you, and certainly don't trust you yet. So, you are only reaching the one percent who already know you and have forgotten that they wanted to check you out the last time they saw your storefront or saw one of your social media posts. This is like playing the advertising game, where you try to build brand awareness by bombarding people with sales messages.

Identify potential partners and then reach out to them with the intention to help them. If you make it about them from the beginning, it's a much easier way to reach out. In the wellness industry, this can be especially useful. People make emotional buying decisions because of your personality and how you interact with them.

It is not necessary to view your fellow practitioner as a competitor just because you use the same or a similar modality or process. There is enough business for everyone, and the right people will buy from you based on who you are, not what you do. Although people come to you because of your expertise, they also buy from you because they like you and trust that you can help them. Both depend on who you are as a person.

Alternative practitioners, therapists, wellness coaches, holistic doctors, and other health, wellness, and lifestyle professionals are potential partners for you. It simply depends on how you think. Having a transactional mindset means you only think about how you can refer to each other and earn commissions in return. A collaborative mindset sees multiple ways in which each of you can help the other grow.

In everything you do in your business, from marketing to sales, employee retention to client retention, always think about how you can help others in a win-win-win way. Often, people overlook their own needs when they are thinking about others' wins, which leads to burnout. Think about how you can create win-win-win situations wherever you go. On my road trips, I talk to café owners, hotel owners, local shop owners, and so forth. My business and mindset revolve around it all the time.

Reach out to potential partners and introduce yourself. Ask them if they would be interested in talking about ways you can work together. You don't need to be awkward here. Imagine if someone asked you that question. What would you do? Given that you are still reading this book, I would assume that you would be quite happy to explore this opportunity. Give it a try if you're still a bit skeptical. It will be a fun and very beneficial process, I promise.

The first action you take together doesn't have to generate tons of leads and new clients. You always start a good relationship one step at a time with patience, no matter how much exposure you get. Creating strategic partnerships is a long-term game that can be both fun and energizing. Fun and energizing conversations are great on their own, but in the long run, strategic partnerships will really take you places.

7.2 – SOCIAL MEDIA

Worldwide, in 2021, every single minute, one million people logged into Facebook, 69 million messages were sent on Facebook Messenger and WhatsApp, 695,00 Instagram stories were shared, 9,132 connections were made on LinkedIn, and 500 hours of content were uploaded on YouTube. The list of these unimaginable numbers goes on. Yes, that's every sixty seconds—every single minute and growing!

The current world seems to revolve around social media. When we look at the younger generation, and how they seem to be looking at their phones all the time, we see how social media is a dominant force in our lives and probably will remain so for a long time. It can be a great platform for businesses to share, but for each of us as individuals, it can be destructive.

As I already mentioned, there are downsides to all this screen time such as the shortened attention span and the inability to simply be in the moment. It is easy to become overwhelmed with all the different platforms, sharing groups, messages, posts, advertisements, and so on within your business. Another detrimental aspect is that you start comparing yourself with others who have played social media games for years. Making comparisons was my worst enemy during my early years. I always thought I wasn't doing enough and I wasn't good enough. Don't fall for that trap. Using these tools effectively is entirely up to you. Learn and find your own path so that you can not only grow your wellness business, but also help the next generation. Help others find a balance between mindfulness in the real world and the ever-expanding digital world.

You can't ignore social media as a marketing channel. You also cannot be sucked in by it all the time, wasting time you could be using elsewhere. It's easy to get distracted on social media. All the platforms tap into your basic human tendencies and suck you into the rabbit hole. Facebook has a whole team whose single job is to research how to take advantage of our basic needs and social behaviors. Tactics like improving the "like" button and notification popups came out of techie labs that explore how far the pull of instant gratification can be taken.

Staying on top of this channel requires getting organized. We need to automate, systematize, and schedule the time we want to spend with this tool of the business. You need to be efficient and focused on your goals without getting distracted.

There are many books written about social media, which I recommend reading if this channel is for you. In this chapter, I will demonstrate how to get started strategically and create some results. I see it go wrong all the time, so even if you are already using social media for your business, you will still benefit from this chapter.

In order to be effective on social media, you firstly need to demonstrate that you are an expert in your field. Secondly, express who you are as a person, and thirdly, understand that the purpose of social media is to get people off it. The latter may sound counterintuitive, but please bear with me.

Let's start with the first one: demonstrating that you are an expert. I think this is the easiest one, but you have to remember that it is about sharing value to educate and not just to sell. All of your content should provide value, such as quick tips, expert interviews, client success stories, and so forth. It's important to mix it up too. People will get bored quickly if they see the same thing over and over again. Many people I work with say, "But I don't know what to write!" even though they have a wealth of knowledge about their field. There is an easy fix for that. All you need is a little trigger to access that knowledge. Try this: Take a piece of paper and a pen; place the paper horizontally in front of you, and write your core expertise in the center. Then write down seven categories around your core expertise, or more if you wish.

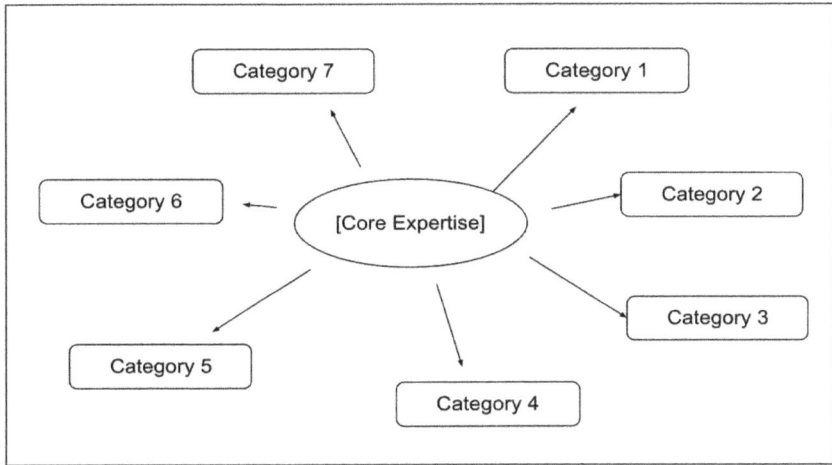

Think outside the box here as well. Not all categories need to relate directly to your core expertise. For example, your core expertise as a family coach might be how to support families with highly sensitive children with learning disabilities. Therefore, you probably also know about nutrition, exercise, fun outdoor activities, toys, educational materials, and the like. Think about what you are interested in and especially your target audience.

Once you have done this, consider the following question: Can you provide a short tip or piece of advice for each of the seven or more categories? This is a powerful practice on many levels. The content found here can be used for newsletters, interviews, blogs, guest articles, short trainings, or any other type of marketing. You can add to this matrix, change it as your expertise grows, and use it as a source of inspiration for future content creation.

We can dive into our second social media foundation, explaining who you are as a person. Social media continues to change the world, and the fact that it influences people to trust people has become more and more crucial as a marketing factor for any business. You can no longer hide behind a brand, as people now want to know who is behind that brand. Having shown that you are an expert in your field, they will want to know more about you as a person. Your beliefs and principles, vision, mission, and values, as well as your personal life, are all important. While you don't have to reveal every detail of your personal life, if you don't disclose any of it, they won't be able to connect with you on a deeper level and, therefore, won't trust you. The more you show who you are as a person, the more people will be able to identify with you and then decide if they want to be a part of what you are offering. Younger generations don't just buy products and services anymore. They want to be part of something bigger than themselves. Many purchase decisions should be guided by sustainability, well-being, equality, and supporting people in need for a better world. A 2019 Deloitte Insight survey[9] showed that "more than 80 percent of consumers would be willing to pay more if a brand raised its prices to be more environmentally and socially responsible or to pay higher wages to its employees." The same survey stated that "...younger generations also want to work at companies with an authentic purpose, with more than 70 percent of millennials expecting their employers to focus on societal or mission-driven problems." This is when your internal and external Why come into play big time. They want to know what your big vision is and how what you do aligns with your mission and values, so that you can fulfill it. You may feel like you're trying to boil the ocean with a Bunsen burner at times, but it's really about letting everyone know that you are doing everything for something much bigger than yourself, your business, and others. People want to be a part of a vision. Toward the end of the book,

---

[9] Diana Obrien, et al, "Purpose is everything: How brands that authentically lead with purpose are authentically changing the nature of business today," Deloitte, 10 October 2019. https://www2.deloitte.com/us/en/insights/topics/marketing-and-sales-operations/global-marketing-trends/2020/purpose-driven-companies.html

we will go into your "Client Attraction Language" where I will run you through steps to create this purpose-driven content that engages with your audience and attracts the right people into your business. For now, you need to understand that no matter what, you have a unique perspective. Share that part of your business. Your story, your values, and your personality can't be replicated by anyone else. Share from the heart and stop pitching your products.

Let me conclude by explaining the third foundation of social media. It's important to do social media to get people off social media. Facebook and Instagram can change their algorithms at any time, or simply shut down due to external factors. There are constant algorithm changes these days, and they can seriously impact your business if you only have an audience on social media. In 2019, Facebook drastically reduced the reach of business pages to put more emphasis on human-to-human interaction through personal profiles, thereby requiring more advertising. Changes like that force you to reevaluate your tactics and strategies constantly.

Because of these changes that social media can and will impose on us, the way to be more in control of your marketing is to capture names and corresponding email addresses. If you have a database of names and emails, you can always download that database and recreate your campaigns on another platform if necessary. You should not underestimate the power of email marketing, which is still one of the most powerful marketing tools out there. Our inboxes seem to be flooded with emails all the time and we might think that people mostly ignore them, but the statistics tell a very different story.

A big piece of the marketing puzzle is not so much about getting someone to read your emails anyway. It's a matter of staying in the front of their mind. Structuring your emails well and focusing on providing valuable content with wit and fun still gets the right people to respond. This leads to a sale.

Considering the uncontrollable changes on social platforms that leave you at the will of big companies like Facebook, LinkedIn, and Twitter, when it comes to communicating with your audience the way you want, your aim on all channels should always be to grow your email database. Remember, you need to use social media to get people off social media. By showing that you are an expert and sharing who you are and what you stand for, you should always lead to a landing page offering people a quick win resource or a Freebie, as we call it in the WPE, in exchange for an email and a name. There are many examples of this strategy on the internet, and you may already be doing this. In light of these social media platforms, it is easy to neglect the importance of sharing and growing your email database. Your business sales can be consistent and predictable despite any changes the platforms can impose. This database allows you to consistently nurture your prospects to take the next step.

As soon as I launched my WPE and posted daily on social media with the intention to provide value, share my personality, and start conversations, I was invited to speak on podcasts, formed great partnerships, and got my first high paying clients through my social media channels.

To stay on top of all this and not get overwhelmed, organize your diary so you can schedule "post creation time" at intervals of your choosing. You can use any frequency that suits you. Also add an hour each week for engaging with people on social media and starting conversations so that you can build relationships.

Of course, you can do more with your social media, but if you want to get started with social media and be strategic with this channel, these three foundational principles will help: Start simple. Don't make it complicated too quickly, and share from your place of purpose, care, and the desire to create change. Get some traction and start creating habits. You can take your time with it. My opinion is that most social media training is too intense and doesn't consider the big picture. Before you can really start, you must get some value from it, and that can only happen if you have your WPE in place and follow some simple steps.

7.3 – YOUR WEBSITE

Our third channel within the WPE is your website. When I talk to people about websites, they already see the website as an important channel for their business. However, there is a reason why the website channel is number three of the five channels in the WPE. Often, when business owners first start a business, they spend a lot of time and money building a website only to realize once it's live that their website gets lost in the vast digital space. So, they study Search Engine Optimization (SEO), Social Media Marketing, advertising, and so forth to try to drive traffic to their websites. Unfortunately, more traffic to your website will not necessarily increase sales if you don't have a proper conversion and sales strategy in place. By focusing on the development of your purpose-driven WPE, you'll be able to build a website that will not only benefit your business, but you'll be able to measure the benefits as well.

I shared this story earlier in the book to demonstrate the importance of creating a program and moving away from a session-by-session approach, but let me pick it up again to explain my points about websites. When we first started our business, we only designed and built websites, nothing else. As soon as we learned how to use a content-management system like WordPress, Squarespace, or Wix, we realized how easy it was to build websites. In 2013, you didn't need any coding skills for most content, and you could obtain the little bit of code you needed via instruction videos on YouTube. Nowadays, due to the development of theme-based website builders, you don't even need that anymore. As a result, there are now over 200 million active websites in the world.[10]

In the past few years, website creation has changed dramatically. I like to compare it to prefabricated houses. In the early 2000s, there were perhaps three designs with very little customization, and changing anything after the house was built was virtually impossible. Say hello

---

[10] Nick Huss, "Resources to Help You Grow Your Online Business and Web Presence," Siteefy, February 16, 2023. https://siteefy.com/how-many-websites-are-there/

to cookie-cutter homes that look like fast food. In 2022, as the fourth generation of the family to live on my parent's land, my sister built a prefabricated home. It is constructed with top-quality materials and a finish that you could not achieve without prefabricating the pieces in an enclosed and controlled environment. Plus, it is fully customized to my sister's family's needs. Brick-by-brick construction is starting to no longer meet the needs of the twenty-first century. The fact alone that the house was constructed in three days in the middle of winter in Germany speaks for itself. It's really amazing.

Websites are similar to this. You can now create a theme-based website that is unique, easy to customize, and has all the bells and whistles you want. It rarely makes sense to hard-code a website from scratch, line-by-line. When theme-based websites first appeared, they were also pretty much cookie-cutter websites. Today, anyone can build a half-decent website. We have seen so many businesses spend tens of thousands of dollars on websites and have nothing to show for the money. Meanwhile, the web gets bigger and noisier very quickly, and the need to cut through that noise becomes more important than ever.

Within our first few months of business, we realized one thing that has stayed with us: People wanted websites because they wanted to grow their businesses. It may seem simple, but that's not what we saw other website agencies and freelancers focusing on. And let's not even mention your Why and what you want to accomplish. This is pretty difficult to do with just a website. We understood that people came to us for a website because they wanted more business, more clients and customers, more revenue and more growth. We wanted to accomplish that for our clients as well, but after doing some research and asking some successful marketers in our early days, we learned that a website alone cannot do all of that.

During the first few years of our business, we would explain to our clients that you have to do more than just build a website. You had to create a full online presence, which included social media, email marketing, search engine optimization (SEO), and marketing (SEM). (We didn't have our WPE back then to explain these needs properly.)

Our clients would agree that they would do all the "additional stuff" after we built the website. Consequently, after the website was completed, we urged them to work with us on their "complete online presence," and their response was always the same: there is not enough money or time for this project right now. Usually after a couple of months, when it was obvious they weren't getting the results from the website, they would call us and ask why they spent all this money with no results. We replied: "We always told you there is more than just building a website."

Our clients were still unhappy even after we reminded them of this. No matter how right we were, it was irrelevant. Only the reality of the customer matters in business! Because we didn't deliver what they wanted, we didn't feel good, and they didn't feel good because they didn't get the results they wanted. Despite being "right", we had lost. We didn't want to do business this way.

At that time, we had no idea how to improve this situation and provide the value our clients needed, and we were very frustrated. As a business, one of our core values has always been integrity. We knew what our clients really wanted, but we didn't seem to be able to deliver because we couldn't get the full commitment from them. In hindsight, I can see that one of the core problems around this issue was that we didn't have the courage to stand up for the work that was necessary to achieve our clients' goals.

The situation is very different now. Instead of making the website the centerpiece of our work, we flipped things on their heads. We developed a program that teaches all the important work first. We show you the benefits of social media, email, content marketing, SEO, how to streamline your business, and so on, with a free website thrown in for good measure.

That is something! As part of a whole system, the website needs only to play a part instead of being the solution for everything. Since then, our clients have loved us. Our clients would still receive a "kick-arse" website and a feeling of value, but they understood they needed to work on their WPE regularly to build their complete online presence, to end up with what they needed.

As time went on, those simple websites became simpler and simpler until finally we decided that instead of a website, all you need to get started is a basic funnel with a few landing pages. In most cases, these funnels are more effective in conjunction with the WPE than the simplest website. This observation doesn't mean you shouldn't build a website. It is my goal to help you understand how to position your website correctly as a channel in your business growth strategy, and how to build it from the ground up. Alternatively, if you already have a website, you can tweak and adapt it in such a way that you will be able to clearly see how it contributes to the bottom line. Let's explore what exactly a funnel is, how to build one and then extend it to a full website with all the bells and whistles you desire.

Everyone knows what a website is, but not everyone understands what a marketing funnel is. Most websites, however, can't be effective without the understanding of a marketing funnel. On a macro level, a marketing funnel consists of three parts: the top of the funnel (TOF), the middle of the funnel (MOF), and the bottom of the funnel (BOF). This is what got drilled into me by my mentor and friend, Michael Griffiths - The Referral Marketing Guru.

Building your audience is at the top of the funnel (TOF), and it's about creating a community of people who need the solution you are offering. If you consistently do this, you will never run out of people to sell to. In the WPE, the top funnel activities are those you carry out through the five channels.

Education is the aim of the middle of the funnel (MOF). By sharing valuable and educational content that helps your audiences, you can build knowledge, familiarity, and trust with your community, so that people in your audience may select themselves and look for the next step to how they can get more from you. This is achieved through all the five channels, but more so with the Freebie and the Entry Product on the left-hand side of the WPE.

In the bottom of the funnel (BOF), you want to get your audience to raise their hands and express that they want to know more about how they can work with you. Most people tend to forget or avoid this part because it feels a bit scary or uncomfortable. However, it is actually quite simple. After you have built an audience and educated it, all you do is to ask who in your audience needs help. Literally. You can do that in a Social Media post, an email, or in a direct message or phone call. Plainly ask: "Would you like some help to achieve … (insert your biggest problem and outcome you achieve for your ideal clients)."

Many people are simply too busy and distracted to pick up the phone and call you or email you, so it's absolutely essential that you ask this question regularly so you give people the opportunity to raise their hands. You can do it in different ways through different channels and mediums, but don't avoid it!

You need to create content for all three parts of this funnel if you want your online marketing and digital business to grow. A website needs to handle all three parts of this marketing funnel.

For those who don't have a website yet, I recommend creating a basic funnel first instead of creating a full website if you're planning to create one.

What do I mean by a basic funnel? Creating a basic funnel involves creating a landing page that is focused on your Freebie, explains a bit about who you are and why you do what you do, and most importantly, convinces people to join your email list in exchange for the Freebie. In the next step, they should be directed to a thank you page inviting them to continue on their Wellness Client Journey, which is the second page you need to create. By doing so, you can build your audience (TOF), educate your audience (MOF), and ask audience members to take the next step (BOF) with a minimum amount of effort. There are many tools out there which allow you to build this basic funnel very quickly. You can then work on building landing pages for all of your different products of your WPE and test what page content works best for your audience. You can check out our example here: www.wellnesspreneur. com.au/map.

No matter if you decide to build a basic funnel first or update your website, content is key. I want to explain to you why your website isn't about you, but about your audience. It is a fact that most websites I come across with potential clients are what I joke about as "an arrogant prick syndrome." I like to make this joke when I teach about websites because I want to really hone in on one of the most important aspects of your website.

Let me explain.

Imagine that you are walking along a beautiful beach promenade. The sun has just begun to set behind the horizon and it's a lovely evening. As you stroll along, you spot a person in the distance. As he or she approaches, you are taken aback, and all you can think is that this could be the person you've been looking for. It's like love at first sight. After thinking about how you can approach him or her, you decide to walk over and just start talking. All you need is a little courage to say "hi". The other person smiles at you and waits for you to say something. You start talking about all the things you do, your skills, your awards, your certificates, and how fantastic you are. After talking for half an hour, you ask the question, "Would you like to marry me?"

Do you think you had much of a chance of finding your life partner with this approach? Most importantly, do you think you behaved a bit like an arrogant prick? Yes? You would never do that, right?

However, if I looked at your website right now, this might be exactly what you are doing. The website of a holistic practitioner or wellness professional is typically a long list of all the different modalities they offer, their certificates, the studies they have completed, and research about how their practices work. There is a lot of content on the website about how great they are. Website pages often conclude with an invitation to "Book now" for a free consultation or discounted session, which is basically asking to get married at the first meeting. Sometimes you may get lucky, but the majority of people simply move on, frustrated or disappointed because they did not feel the connection. Of course, none of this comes from a place of arrogance. In a world where western medicine is the norm and holistic practices are often falsely judged, it is understandable that many practitioners feel they need to prove themselves with lots of content. The Book Now offer is then a step that is simply too great a leap.

People go online to solve a problem. Always! Whether you are looking up a restaurant because you don't want to cook that day or you are looking to finally solve that health issue you have been struggling with for years, you have a problem and you want to solve it. Finding a takeaway restaurant is pretty straightforward and it may take a couple of minutes. On the other hand, solving a long-term health issue is very different. The bigger the problem, the longer the Wellness Client Journey might be and the more important for you to make sure you have your WPE in place so you can take people on that journey.

Don't get me wrong. It's important to state your credentials but don't make this the main focus. Keep it short, sharp, and concise.

Remember, people are browsing online and thinking, "What's in it for me" (WII FM). With any online content you create, you must tune it to the radio station WII FM. People don't care how Google Maps calculates their route or how their birthday present is manufactured before it's delivered to their doorstep. They don't care how someone fixes their car or health issue. They just want it fixed. People are interested in how you can help them with a possible solution to the problem they have.

In general, there are three types of people who visit your website. The first type of person is "the Researcher". This person conducts research on what you do and simply collects information. Most of those people can be ignored as they don't help your business to grow.

The second type are those who already know you. Let's call them "the Acquaintance". They may have met you at a networking event, seen your videos and posts on social media, or heard you speak at an event. In some form, they have consumed enough content through the other channels to have a specific question or need about your business. They will head to your website to find the answer, look at the menu, and navigate to the information they require. This might be to book a call with you, sign up for your newsletter, or download a guide.

As a result, you should only worry about the third type of person, "the Seeker", when you create the content for your website pages or funnel. Seekers usually find your website on Google, social media, or any other website online and are looking for a solution to their problem. They are seeking answers to a specific need.

Pages like About, Contact, or Blog have specific requirements that are mostly straightforward, and you should consider what I am about to tell you for all pages. Your home page is critical for probably 90 percent of Seekers because that is where they land first.

Consider a scenario where a Seeker lands on your home page and you go on and on about how amazing you are without clearly showing that you have what they are looking for. Plus, all you might ask them to do is to call you. What will that person do?

Most likely, they'll be disappointed and leave your site quickly. How can you avoid this behavior? Listen to WII FM. Tune into what your visitor is looking for by answering *their* question: "What's in it for me?" List the problems you solve to show that you understand their struggle. Afterward, provide them with the outcomes you offer and only then describe the features of your solution and how they benefit your clients. If someone wakes up in the morning feeling sore or with very low energy, they don't think, "I really need someone to pull my left leg to do a muscle test so I can understand my inner child better." No, they think, "If only there would be someone who gets me and can show me how I can have more energy throughout my day and finally get a good night's sleep." Get clear on the problems you solve, the outcomes you generate, and the benefit-rich solutions that bridge the two, and then put that on your home page or landing page. Fill it in with testimonials, your own story, logos from universities and organizations you have worked with, and degrees and certificates you have earned, but don't make that the majority of your content.

This will avoid the arrogant prick syndrome! However, if you still ask to marry someone at first sight, you reduce your chance of building a relationship. So don't ask to book a free consultation on your home page. That's basically saying "Book in a call where I will sell you my stuff." The same goes for asking your visitors to call or email you. In other words, these type of "calls to action" are saying "marry me"!

This doesn't mean you shouldn't have contact forms and booking systems on your website, just don't make them the focal point of your home page. Think about the problem each page is designed to solve, as well as the outcomes and benefits it will provide. Consider the reasons why people would end up on the page you are creating, tune in to WII FM, and then create and structure the content for the page accordingly. Add a Call to Action at the end of each page. Your Call to Action should be the next step in your WPE. Usually this is your Freebie or Entry Product.

Depending on where your visitor is on their journey, your Call to Action should suggest the next step for them. The visitors who scroll through your home page are at the beginning of their journey, so your Freebie should be the Call to Action. You can have a free Clarity Conversation on your service or product page, or you might even have a questionnaire or self-test that leads into a call. Always end a page and any type of longer content with a Call to Action. Make it easy to take action. They've just read some inspiring content, and you may have given them hope that they have finally discovered a solution to their problem. Give them the next step!

One of my clients was featured in a well-known and widely distributed local magazine. She wanted to tell the whole story of how she became a fertility coach. This was a great story and the article was well written. Creating this article required a great deal of work and time. Before and after the article's release, her excitement was through the roof. Having seen the article, I reviewed it for her. I enjoyed reading it, but when I reached the end, my excitement quickly dwindled. I couldn't find any information about how to contact her – no social media tags, no email, no contact number, nothing. Her full name was not even included in the article because they had used her shortened nickname.

There it was: an article that told her story beautifully and really engaged the reader by introducing who she was and what her business was all about. The problem was that there was no name to search for, no Call to Action, and therefore no opportunity for anyone to take the next step. Sure, readers could contact the magazine for more information, but who is going to jump over that hurdle? She was very disappointed when I pointed all of this out to her.

It is really a shame that so many media outlets don't think about these issues and provide appropriate advice. I am not suggesting making a landing page out of an article with a hundred calls to action. There are very elegant ways of giving the reader the opportunity to reach out and take the next step. A simple profile picture with a short description and your full name with a link to your website inviting the reader to get more information is more than enough.

Again, it is your job to ensure that the content you create leads into the next step of the Wellness Client Journey. I cannot emphasize enough how important this is. It takes time and effort to create content that engages the reader and makes an impact, so you can't afford to not make any sales from it. The content may educate and even inspire the audience, but to keep this kind of information flowing, you need to make sure you get something in return that makes it all worthwhile.

Don't hesitate to contact the magazine or the radio station to find out which opportunities they provide to promote your business or yourself in the content piece they are looking to feature. They need great content all the time, and you should make it a win-win situation for both of you. Be courageous and stand tall. It is truly valuable to hear what you have to say. You should be proud of that.

If you have this mindset and follow the strategies and principles above, you will transform any website into a valuable piece of your business. Websites don't need fancy SEO, great advertising, or exceptional designers in order to succeed. It is crucial to understand that your website is not about you but is all about providing a solution to someone's problem while telling a great story. You should ensure that your content reflects this.

7.4 – EVENTS

The fourth channel of the WPE is the events channel. It is my favorite channel, and it closely relates to all the other channels mentioned above. Specifically, it's often an extension of the partner channel. When you find the right people to partner with, it becomes natural for you to propose, invite, be invited, or create your own events, such as speaking gigs, interviews, and workshops. Events can be speaking events, guesting on other people's podcasts, workshops, and retreats, anywhere you can share your expertise and story with a group of people that is not your own audience.

Speaking and presenting to many people at once is the essence of the event channel. This can range from a brief presentation to ten people during a networking event to large online conferences or webinars to hundreds or thousands of people.

While you can pick up new business with the other three channels – partners, social media, and your website – the last two, events and advertising, strongly rely on the system. I suggest you build and tweak your basic funnel using the first three channels and then build your WPE from there. Once you figure out your own way and what works best for your business, you can use the event channel to take your business to the next level.

You need to take time to understand your marketing objectives for the different channels in order to leverage this channel to its full potential. Don't act out of desperation or unnecessary urgency. As Stephen Covey wrote in his book *The 7 Habits of Highly Effective People,* "Begin with the end in mind." This premise can be applied to other aspects of your life or any project or strategy you wish to implement. In fact, activities without a clear end in mind are often ineffective, hoping for a successful outcome instead of fully taking responsibility for everything you do. Think strategically about what you do. Always! Even if you speak with a large number of people, there is still the possibility of leaving a lot of money on the table if you do not have a strategic approach. It takes a lot of effort to plan, organize, show up and run an event, as well as handle all the aftermath. The bigger the event, the bigger the effort. For example, when you present during a one-week online conference where dozens of speakers are present, you must make sure you understand the audience, what you can do to follow up, and provide further materials for those who are interested in what you discussed.

Let's ensure you know exactly how to effectively prepare and grow your business with events. One of the most important ways to be prepared is to understand your audience. The three types of people that you typically find at an event are as follows. About 40 to 60 percent are just curious about the topic or are there as part of a larger event. These people are not ready for your solution and are very unlikely to take any action after listening to you. They typically need at least another three to six months to explore your products further through other channels and consume a lot more content from you before they will be ready to work with you. Many of them may never be ready.

The second group of people, about 37 to 58 percent, are those who come interested and half-ready. They saw a potential solution to their problem in your topic. Nevertheless, they are at the beginning of their journey with you and will require more valuable information before they will consider working with you.

The third group comprises people who have been waiting and were ready yesterday, making up about 2 to 3 percent of your audience. Their interest in what you offer is great and they have probably seen other videos, articles, and social media posts. They might even be on your email list, follow you on social media, or have read a good deal of content on your website before the event. You already have a relationship with these people, so they are ready for more.

When it comes to using this channel correctly, it comes down to remembering the first step along the Wellness Client Journey or in other words, the first and lowest risk offer in the WPE – the Freebie. This is the best way for you to capture the first two groups, which account for over 90 percent of your audience.

If you are invited to speak at a conference, podcast interview, or seminar that gives you the opportunity to tap into other people's audience, you need to learn how to weave your Freebie into the conversation or presentation script. It is a valuable quick-win and low-risk offer that appeals to people from all three groups. As they become more aware of the problem you can solve for them, anyone signing up for Freebies will receive more valuable content to further explore how you can help them.

This is not the place to offer introductory sessions or special discounts for your Featured Product. A lot of people make this mistake when using the events channel.

This is not the case when your event is specifically about your Feature Product. Suppose, for example, you give a half-day seminar about a subject that comes under your expertise or program and leads into a sales call or pitch in the afternoon. In this case, your event is not a channel but rather acts as an Entry Product that serves as a stepping stone in your WPE. There's a very significant difference between the events channel and an event being part of your sales. In this case you use the event to sell your product, not build your audience.

Build this clarity and confidence with your business system so that all you have to do is share your expertise and little nuggets of gold here and there for someone to take the first step on their journey toward working with you. It takes some trial and error to get to this point, but once you do, it will be a lot of fun. You will no longer worry about making a sale right away and simply share your passion with enthusiasm and joy.

Getting your products out there with joy and great energy will make you have fun with your digital and offline activities like your events. When you focus on doing that, the sales will follow. Eventually, everything will start to flow for you, and chances will start popping up everywhere. This is my favorite stage. I love doing podcast interviews, feature articles, and presentations to share my free resources online and then seeing a bunch of signups pop up in my inbox, which lead into bookings for a Clarity Conversation, where I talk with people one-on-one about my Feature Product.

Often, we miss opportunities because we are too focused on making a sale and are too deep in the operations of the business because we don't have systems and processes in place that allow us to think freely and creatively about everything we experience on a daily basis. In our business, we should create joy and freedom so that we can enjoy ourselves again like kids going to a fair. Do you remember that? You arrive at the fair and are so excited you can't decide what to do first. Let's be that kid again when it comes to business. Your inner journey has a lot to do with this, but you have to also build systems and processes first so that you will develop the mindset, be curious like a kid, and freely share your authentic self and transformational expertise through all the different channels in your business.

12

PAID PROMOTION

Aʜ, ʜᴏᴡ I "ʟᴏᴠᴇ" this channel. Paid promotion or advertising is the very last channel you should implement. It can be a great way to amplify what you know already works in your business, but don't try to use this as a quick fix to get sales. I have seen it go wrong too many times. Once you understand the numbers of your business, you can strategically and with confidence use this channel effectively. What do I mean by that? When you have your WPE or even your basic funnel in place, you can start measuring how many people need to go through your Wellness Client Journey within your WPE to make a sale. This is absolutely essential for this channel because, unless you know those numbers, you are walking in the dark, hoping for the best. As I said before: "Hope is not a good business strategy." It's dangerous. Use your other four marketing channels first to understand your numbers, and then consider paid promotion.

Years ago, when I was a newbie to business, I spent a total of $2,000 on Facebook advertising without seeing any return. Yes, that's correct, $0 return. During my lowest point, I desperately needed new clients. To help me out, I hired a large marketing agency to do some Facebook advertising for me. After they promised me the world, I took on a three-month package that required me to pay for the Facebook ads budget as well as for creating and managing the ads. I got nothing out of it. They did not deliver on their promises. Even though I did not end up paying the agency because I refused for several weeks until they gave up, I still couldn't recuperate the cost of $2,000 for the Facebook ad budget. Don't make the same mistake.

Don't get me wrong, there are some excellent marketing agencies out there who, if you can afford them, will skyrocket your business. However, many do not take the time to understand the unique aspects of a client in order to produce a strategy and a plan that is aligned fully with the client's needs. Instead, clients are often given a generic campaign. The only person who can truly understand your ideal client is you, and only you have the right information to attract this ideal client. It's important to have someone to extract this information from you and transform it into a structure and process that works. Any company that asks you what you want advertised, and then goes ahead and does it without proper consultation and proper assessment of your individual needs, will not get you results. It's similar to you selling your clients a treatment plan or medicine the minute they walk in the door, without any assessment or consultation.

This is again one of the reasons why your WPE is so powerful. Everything you do online can be tracked, allowing you to measure everything exactly to the smallest detail. On a basic level, for example, let's say you know that 100 downloads of your Freebie convert into 40 people accessing your Entry Product. This may be 100 people downloading a simple "How-to-guide" and then 20 people buying a three-part online course for $49. Five of those 40 people will book a conversation with you, resulting in three sales, each worth $1,000. Based on this understanding, you can calculate the value of 100 Freebie downloads at $3,980 [(3 x $1000) + (20 x $49)].

The old me, who spent $2,000 on Facebook ads, would have advertised the $1,000 product. It was a revelation to me to understand the power of the WPE and how it can help you get the results you want without wasting thousands of dollars on advertising. It is much easier to advertise a Freebie than a $1,000 product. Imagine you would know exactly how much you need to spend to get those 100 Freebie downloads or how much effort you would need to put into your other marketing channels to achieve those 100 downloads! Advertising and business are numbers games at their core, so to succeed you need to understand your numbers.

In contrast to online marketing and advertising, TV, radio, and newspaper ads are very challenging. A newspaper or magazine will try to get you to run ads in their prints by showing you how many copies they sell. They tell you they sell 10,000 or even more than 100,000 copies and you think "wow that's a lot of people I can reach," but how many of those copies just lie around waiting rooms and nobody reads them? What percentage of readers read only the front page? How many people only read the articles and never look at your advertisement? Without a unique number or email setup for that ad, you will never know. This is the reason I generally steer clear of print advertising.

Implement the paid promotion channel last. Put your focus on the other four channels first to make your WPE work like a well-oiled machine. This will enable you to make enough revenue to afford good advertising, and you will be able to work with almost any agency or freelancer to take your business to the next level.

You need to make this channel an extension of all the others. The approach should not stand alone, but rather be used to enhance what is already working. You can generate an exciting number of sales if you leverage your knowledge and expertise through strategic partners, social media, your website, and events. In no time, you will not only have your head above water, but also grow your influence and impact. Now there is only one part left to talk about to fully implement your WPE.

13

SALES

So, you've finally worked through all the marketing channels. Go you! You've drummed up interest, people have been attracted to your Freebie, some have fallen away, and some have gone on to invest time, money, or both into your Entry Product. Now it's time for you to focus on the sale of your Feature Product. As your prospects have gone through the first steps in their Wellness Client Journey, you have enough "know, like and trust" so that they become presold customers. At this point, you need to get them over the line with a genuine conversation, which I call a Clarity Conversation. In this chapter, I will show you a sales system and process that gets the right people to book this Clarity Conversation and positions you as the expert in your niche while converting a high percentage without being salesy or pushy.

Most people find selling uncomfortable, so they hide behind the front desk at a clinic or avoid it by having a "coffee catch up". Please don't do that! Put yourself in charge of this vital aspect of your business. You can implement the sales system I am about to show you, one step at a time. Feel into it, and adapt it to fit your needs. Even with the perfect WPE in place, it's very difficult to sell your Feature Product without a sales system.

This Sales Process has two simple steps:

1. Qualifying
2. Clarity Conversation

Before we get into this two-step process, I want to make sure you understand how people make decisions, as this is fundamental for both steps.

It is important to understand that people buy emotionally and then justify logically. It is in that moment between seeing something and purchasing it that you anticipate how it will feel to have it.

Buying a car is a good example of this. You sit in the car and take it for a test drive. As you drive this brand-new car, you feel the thrill and excitement of experiencing something new like new features, a new design, a new feel, and a brand-new drive. All these features add to your excitement and tempt you to make the purchase.

It doesn't mean you don't think about whether you can afford a new car, but at this stage of prepurchasing, your emotions are in charge. At this point, people often choose to get the top-of-the-line model over the basic one, even though logically the additional features may be overpriced and unnecessary.

In my first couple of years in Australia, I was surprised to see so many top-of-the-line German cars. I wondered what happened to the simple VW Golfs or the entry-level Mercedes with standard engines and interiors. It seems that in Australia you can only find the GTI Golf with 230 horsepower and double turbo or the Mercedes AMG with a 6.3l engine that produces close to 500 horsepower. With cars such as these, you could take on anyone on the renowned public racetrack at Nürburgring in Germany, the Nordschleife, the most prestigious racetrack in the world where supercars are tested and compared to each other, and where anyone can drive on it for a small fee. I am a bit of a car enthusiast, as you may have noticed. Those top-spec cars in Australia seem a bit ridiculous, considering the highway speed limit in Australia is

110 km/hour and most curvy roads have a 60 km/hour limit. They seem to cruise at 40 km/hour in the inner city or are always stuck in traffic.

So, why do people choose to buy these cars in the first place? Certainly, it isn't rational for people to pay absurdly high prices for these cars. It's the emotion and feeling of prestige and what you might potentially be able to do with the car when you put your foot down. After you drive home with your new car and drive it around for a while, those feelings of "I really want this" quickly fade, and you start to justify your purchase. After you've bought the car emotionally, you justify it logically. You might say things like: "There's no doubt about it, I love the sound of this powerful engine and the sound system is awesome. I really enjoy listening to music while driving and it makes me happy." Or, "With the camping trip we might go on soon, and the fact that I sometimes need to transport heavy items from the hardware store, this SUV is great for us." Our purchase continues to be justified logically.

The point I'm making is that your sales shouldn't be based solely on the logical features of your Feature Product, but rather on the emotional factors that drive a purchase. You are about making people feel better. That's what people really want at their core. Focusing on their problems and outcomes is the best way to elicit those emotional factors which support the decision-making process.

If you can identify and verbalize where your prospects are and what they are looking for, and then briefly outline how your solution bridges the gap, you will tap into those emotions. To do this, you must get to the bottom of your prospect's problems and the resulting fears if they don't address these problems, as well as their dreams that are beyond their wants. Whenever you inquire about someone's current situation and why they are here with you today, most people will only share their superficial problems and wants. If you are an osteopath, for example, as a client I might mention that I have some knee pain and would like to resolve it. Your response might be, "Thank you, let me assess you," and then you treat me and probably tell me to continue to book more sessions until it is resolved.

The above potentially leaves at least 40 percent of the money on the table and won't resolve my real issue. For my dream was not to get rid of the pain but to be able to run 10k again and train for an IronMan or marathon. I was worried that I would never be able to do that or that the pain would get worse so that I couldn't even play soccer with my friends or kids.

That is where the emotion resides. You have to look deeper and discover why your client wants to end the pain and what is blocking them from achieving what they really want and dream of. Only then will it be a no-brainer to buy your "10-week transformational health program" for example. When I get answers to my basic sales questions, I say "why" and "tell me more". The moment I understand why the person is really talking to me, I feel like I have connected with the person and the real underlying issue. That is when I have the opportunity to sell my high-ticket transformational Feature Product. I believe sales is about patient care and the opportunity to transform someone's life. You can accomplish this if you delve deeply into someone's emotions and desires, their Why, making a deeper connection than a transactional exchange. Don't "just fix the knee." Instead, help me live my healthiest and happiest life.

As soon as you start to understand how people make decisions, you can use that knowledge not only in your sales but also your marketing channels and Wellness Client Journey. Sales is not about manipulating anyone, but removing yourself from what you think is best for your clients and diving deeply into their desires, so you can determine what they need to fulfill them. The results will be transformational, the money highly profitable, and your opportunities to refer, collaborate, and partner with others, exceptional. You will not be playing the fixing game, rather you will be playing the empowering game in which you take someone's hand and support their journey to wellness, happiness, and joy.

Now that you fundamentally understand how people make decisions, let's talk about how you can implement this two-step sales process. The first step is called "Qualifying". A highly efficient and high-converting sales process relies on qualifying your prospect before explaining your program or service. This first step is about making sure that your prospect knows you are the expert and that they are ready to take action. Otherwise, you have a much higher chance of wasting your time by explaining your Feature Product to the wrong people.

You want to work with those persons who care and align with you, not those who are looking for the cheapest deal. To find the right people quickly, you check where your prospect is currently in their life, where they want to go, and if what you offer is the missing link to get them there. This is the essence of Qualifying. Whenever someone asks to talk to you, invite them to a fifteen-minute call by saying, "Let's have a brief fifteen-minute call to learn more about where you are, where you want to go, and how we can help you get there." Depending on your product, you can customize this invitation and make it your own.

The name of the call should be enticing. Do not call it a Qualifying Call – no one wants to book that. Create an "Empathic Leadership Call" or a "Family Joy Call", something that will pique interest. During the call, ask them how things look in their life/business/work now, and where they see themselves in six weeks, three months or a year, and what they think is missing or holding them back. You should ask "why" for every answer, or "tell me more" until you feel like you really have connected and they have honestly shared what's behind their answers.

You then ask them whether they would prefer to take action sooner or later. Usually, it is "sooner" and you can book in step two of your sales process, your Clarity Conversation. Make this a separate conversation. Don't be tempted to go straight into the Clarity Conversation or to talk about features and specifics of your Feature Product. Your clients booked a fifteen-minute call, so you need to honor that. Ask if they would like to discover how you can accomplish together what you explored in the qualifying step. The Clarity Conversation is a second and longer conversation. Book this appointment before concluding the call.

If they say "later", you have the option of setting up a time to follow up or recommend a different practitioner or modality. It's likely that after this conversation, you can actually refer them to someone more suitable, since you now understand more clearly what would help them. Ideally, you have a strategic partner that you could refer to. Like a GP refers to a specialist, but with the difference that you create a win-win every time you refer. Imagine the impact of your referrals!

As a result of Qualifying, you not only get to speak to the right people, but you also save a lot of time. You can use the Qualifying Call Sheet that I use to easily run these conversations. This sheet can be downloaded from the resources section of the book. (www.wellnesspreneur. com.au/book-resources)

In step two, your Clarity Conversation, you want your prospect to be on board for the entire journey, not just a part of it but the whole transformational program from beginning to end. In this step, you can finally state clearly what you have to offer with all the features, logistics, and bells and whistles. At this point in the Wellness Client Journey, your prospects understanding your value and are ready to make a purchase. They have already been pre-sold. They only need a little more trust by making a personal connection with you and clearly understanding what and how you will deliver. The goal isn't to convince or manipulate someone into buying, but to create clarity about the value and logistics of your product and services. Because of this, I prefer calling this a Clarity Conversation rather than a sales conversation.

Let me take you through the different parts of your Clarity Conversation. The first thing you want to do before providing any details about your product or service is to put the prospect in the right emotional state again. Remember that people make decisions emotionally. Pull out your notes from the Qualifying Call and identify the problems and wants of your prospect, so you can tap into the fears and dreams behind them. Dig deeper than in the short Qualifying Call and really get your prospect excited about the opportunity to finally solve their problems and live a better life. Show your own excitement about this and lift your client's emotional state.

A very common mistake people make in sales is that they talk about the features and logistics of what they do the moment someone shows interest in working with them. Among other things, they talk about how many treatments, how many video calls, how many workbooks, what happens at a session, and what is in the private Facebook group. When you do that without qualifying and getting people excited about your solutions, the features don't matter. On the other hand, if you connect with someone on an emotional level, you can clearly demonstrate the value of what you do and not be judged solely on your price.

To achieve this, you want to start by what is called lowering buyer resistance. Let your prospect tell you why your product is so important to them right now, what they are struggling with, and what they really want. You may even mention other clients you've worked with who had similar struggles and how working with you transformed their businesses or lives. This approach always opens up prospects and reduces resistance to what you have to offer. Understanding the most common challenges that people need to overcome before buying your product and forming questions and stories around them which you can weave into the conversation is a great idea here.

If money is an issue, for instance, make a list of your success stories, where previous clients had the same issue and how they made the money work through a payment plan, and how they've never looked back after the exceptional investment they made in their health.

After lowering buyers resistance, you need to increase buyers acceptance by showing them the path they can take and how it will help them achieve the wants and dreams they have expressed. Your ideal clients will naturally express needs, fears, and desires that perfectly match your product. When this happens, it is quite magical. If you acknowledge and think about the process you have taken them through to get to this point, and the hurdles they had to jump over, how can it be any other way?

It's really important that you remind them why they have gone through all these different steps to get here. What are the real reasons behind the problems and fears? What do they fear in the future if they don't solve their problems, and what do they dream to have in their lives? That's where the emotion is. That's what really matters. That's where you need to get to before you talk about all the great things in your Feature Product.

Their problems and fears will create a clear picture of where your prospect is in their life right now, and the wants and dreams represent where they want to go. All you need to do now is to show them a plan on how to get there. One of the easiest ways to demonstrate a clear plan or pathway forward is to provide your prospect with a visual representation. People can more easily understand and connect with something when they can see it. Accompanying visuals aid retention, meaning your prospects will understand and remember your solution much more easily. I have a hard time understanding concepts if they are explained with facts and figures alone and in great detail. However, if I have a story or a visual to accompany them, I understand them much more easily.

For instance, I use the WPE model in my Clarity Conversation. I show my prospect how creating products will benefit their wellness business, which products to automate, and how to use the five marketing channels more effectively so they can grow their business. I relate all of this to the problems and fears they express, as well as the goals and dreams they have with their business.

The moment you have a visual and put it in front of your prospect, it becomes real, understandable, and memorable. The information is presented directly in front of them so they can see it clearly. Ultimately, you need to communicate how each step will help them achieve their goals and change their lives for the better. Check out the book resources for how you can create your own unique model or graphic for your Feature Product. (www.wellnesspreneur.com.au/book-resources)

Don't hesitate to share your best tools and advice with your prospect to guide them through your plan, model, and the pathway to their wants and dreams. Success for your prospects depends on more than simply following the steps or taking advice, and your ideal clients will know that. What makes the difference at the end is the accountability and wisdom you provide along the journey.

When you have done all of the above, you have overcome almost any obstacle for the sale. Now the transformational value you provide is crystal clear. At this point, your prospect is longing for the information on how to make it all happen. It's clear how your product will help them and they can also see how they would need you to implement it.

All of the above – the lowering of buyers resistance, the increasing of buyers acceptance, and demonstrating the plan – is all about putting your prospect into that emotionally heightened state. It's that test drive of the new car before purchase. Now it's finally time to talk about all the features and how you are going to deliver on your promises. Ask your prospect if they want to know how you can work together to achieve this plan and watch how they react. They can't wait for you to tell them. Give them a thorough explanation of the features and the logistics of your solution. Describe the actual tangibles they'll receive. Identify how many sessions, private Facebook groups, workbooks, accountability buddies, virtual meetups with the community, or workshops your Feature Product includes. The more you break it down and the more you list, the better. You will greatly increase the value of your solution if you are able to demonstrate how each item contributes towards the pathway you outlined and achieving the goals that you discussed.

After that, it's time to ask your prospect to make a decision. Offer either-or options and ask which one will suit them best instead of just asking "what they think?" At this point, no more thinking is needed. Both of you have thought about it enough. Now it's time to make a decision. Ask something like: "Would you prefer the do-it-yourself option for $497 or the one-on-one coaching for $4,997 dollars? What suits you best?" This way, it's much easier to create a positive outcome. You can test it on yourself. Imagine you are confronted with making a purchase decision and are asked the questions above. How does it make you feel? It's much different from asking what you think about it, isn't it? Make sure you book the first session of your Feature Product or whatever the first simple step is for them to get started. You can say something like: "Great, let's get you started by booking in your first session and I will email you with the formalities such as the payment process and the agreement."

Understanding decision making and implementing the two-step sales process of Qualifying and Clarity Conversation has allowed me to achieve a sales conversion rate of over 80 percent. I look forward to each Clarity Conversation because I know the people I will be talking to are fully aligned and ready to work with me. If you want to build a successful business, you must be strategic about how you sell, and the WPE with all its steps is a fantastic way to do that.

A few last words on Sales. Make sure you have a qualification step as well as a run sheet for your Clarity Conversation that outlines the basic structure and questions you'll ask. Also, make it easy for the prospect to schedule time with you by setting up an online calendar. Scripts and templates can feel a bit robotic at first but, once they are part of how you do things in your business, they are powerful frameworks and spaces where you can be creative.

The sales process, and even everything before that in your WPE, are about helping your ideal client to move forward on their Wellness Client Journey and not about attempting to close the sale. It is true that the structure of this process is designed in a way that it sells well, but the attitude behind it is about providing value and having a great conversation with a person you really care about.

Do you remember the "arrogant prick syndrome" we talked about earlier in the book when it came to your website? The same principle applies here. Don't tell them how great you are and then ask if they want to marry you. Make it about them and learn everything you can about their needs. After that, you can suggest what you believe the two of you can accomplish together, which will be a much more harmonious and successful marriage.

You will play a role as a guide, not a dictator. It is as if you are Gandalf guiding Frodo in *The Lord of the Rings* or Obi Wan Kenobi guiding Luke Skywalker in *Star Wars*. Being a wise guide means trusting that the right people will make the right decisions and decide what's best for them. In this way, the most interesting and beautiful things will emerge. Let things happen as they need to within the basic framework of the WPE and your sales process.

The success of your business depends on sales; therefore, all of your marketing campaigns and activities should center on your sales process. You can't grow your business without sales, and without growth you won't have impact. Like every living thing on earth, you either grow or you die. It may sound harsh, but it is true. In some way or another, you must grow on the inside, outside, or at best, both. The purpose of sales is to give you the space, energy and resources to do exactly that. Sales is the lifeblood of your business growth.

As long as you follow the steps outlined in this book, there is no need to put immense pressure on anyone, either the prospect or yourself. The WPE allows you to be your true authentic self and share your unique story unapologetically from the heart. You will connect with others deeply during this process and gain a greater understanding of yourself and your work, which is the path to success.

PART IV

Getting Started

INTRODUCTION

ADDRESSING THAT AGE-OLD QUESTION

"The way to get started is to quit talking and begin doing."

—Walt Disney

AFTER ALL WE HAVE COVERED, the question remains: "Where do I get started?"

The majority of business owners I come across find it difficult to connect with their market, tell their story, and use the systems and processes to increase sales and make the impact they desire. The best systems and strategies in the world are completely useless if you don't know what creates an emotional connection with your audience.

It is imperative that you assemble all the different stories, your connections, and the people around you in a way that all your content shared by you and your peers delivers the same powerful message.

It is important for people to identify with a brand. You can do this in your own small or big way by sharing the people behind the brand and what they stand for. If it's just you and your business, start there and add the client success stories as you go.

First and foremost, you should determine what the content is. In what ways and how does information really connect with people? What interests them, what taps into their emotions? Knowing the answers to these questions will create a real connection with people so that you can educate them and create loyal customers.

I call this your "Marketing Engagement Language". It is the voice of your brand that people will hear or read when they encounter your brand. People trust people, and marketing is a human-to-human approach to changing behavior. This Language must be developed specifically for you, and you must find influencers that people already trust to promote it. This is the first step in combining your Inner and Outer Game. Connect with the people that align with your purpose and your Why by developing strategic partnerships.

With the clarity of your language and brand voice combined with increased exposure from trusted influencers and existing customers, we can educate and establish your brand as a go-to solution in your niche.

To manage your client-related tasks efficiently and effectively, you will need a system that you can build with the WPE. Before we can build this system, we will need to build a strong foundation. By placing your Marketing Engagement Language at the core of all your business activities, you can achieve freedom, flow, and fulfillment.

You are already standing on a mighty mountain of value. To understand the value of your mountain, you need to look down at it. When you look at all the other mountains and compare yourself with others, you forget that your path is unique. Comparing it with others' paths will only create feelings of inferiority and stress.

Here I will detail how to determine your Marketing Engagement Language and identify your strategic partners so you can share your real value with the world. By doing this, you will be able to determine your niche and how you need to communicate with your ideal clients.

Creating your Marketing Engagement Language may well be one of the most important activities you do for your business. Throughout this book, everything is built on this critical step in your business development. You need your Marketing Engagement Language to grow your wellness business. As soon as you have a clear understanding of your Marketing Engagement Language, everything else will flow from there.

This process was designed to help you put your heart and soul into it and come up with marketing language that you will feel proud to use. Regardless of how well you write, it may require courage to share the results at first, no matter how well they sit with you.

However, the results will be stunning, and it will become second nature to you after you begin using your new language. I always get excited about this part. So, let's do it!

1

YOUR "WHY"

"When the roots are deep, there is no reason to fear a storm."

—African Proverb

ACTIVITY #3 - YOUR WHY

IF YOU HAVE READ THIS book front to back, you may have already done the exercise in the first section of the book, the Inner Game, and the Internal and External Why in chapter three. I suggest that you return to that chapter, read what you have written there again, and then write an updated version below. If you haven't done the exercise in that chapter, I urge you to create the space for this task now and take action.

The language you use for marketing engagement is a continuous process that requires regular refinement. Your target audience changes ever so slightly and sometimes may even take a big leap and change completely as you grow your business. This is a process I revisit regularly to keep my inner and outer being in alignment. Growth takes place within and without, so it is essential to constantly move between the two.

Your External Why:

_____

_____

_____

_____

_____

_____

_____

_____

_____

_____

Your Internal Why:

_____

_____

_____

_____

_____

_____

_____

_____

_____

_____

_____

2

LIVING YOUR VALUES

*"A highly developed values system is like a compass.
It serves as a guide to point you in the right direction
when you are lost."*

—Idowu Koyenikan

YOUR PERSONAL WHY AND the resulting vision for your business combined with your three core values will make you unstoppable! The three core values you choose to live by will tell you how to make more aligned and authentic decisions to stay on your purpose-driven path or when to choose a new one. Values are the guiding principles by which we live our lives. If life is a journey up a long and treacherous mountain and your vision is a guiding star, then our values are our guides that help us to safely navigate the terrain and find the best path forward. They help to keep us in check and can be the tools we use to create situations in our lives that lead us to be in states of flow, joy, and love.

Truly living who you are is an admirable goal, but it is not an easy one. We all enjoy positive values like integrity, honesty, happiness, and so on, but what are the values that make up your deepest self? Are there three core values that you can fully trust that will be congruent with who you are if you make decisions based on them? As soon as you align everything you do, the universe will give way and take you on a wonderful journey. You will stay true to yourself and find joy in what you do as you stay true to your core values.

Your business values may be different from your personal values. It is important that you create a different set of values with your employees as they will guide everyone in your business and not just yourself. At this time, our focus is on your personal values which will help you grow, but you can use this process as many times as you like to cocreate the values for your business with your employees.

ACTIVITY #4 - YOUR VALUES

Start by circling twenty values that you think are close to your heart in the list below:

Authenticity	Fame	Peace
Achievement	Friendships	Pleasure
Adventure	Fun	Poise
Authority	Growth	Popularity
Autonomy	Happiness	Recognition
Balance	Honesty	Religion
Beauty	Humor	Reputation
Boldness	Influence	Respect
Compassion	Inner Harmony	Responsibility
Challenge	Justice	Security
Citizenship	Kindness	Self-Respect
Community	Knowledge	Service
Competency	Leadership	Spirituality
Contribution	Learning	Stability
Creativity	Love	Success
Curiosity	Loyalty	Status
Determination	Meaningful Work	Trustworthiness
Fairness	Openness	Wealth
Faith	Optimism	Wisdom

Add any other values that you feel drawn to and are not listed above:

_____

_____

_____

_____

_____

_____

_____

_____

_____

_____

_____

_____

Imagine yourself on a lonely island and the only way to be rescued is to climb up that mountain in the middle. You packed all of the twenty values you circled above and each value weighed one kilogram. You realize halfway up the mountain that it's just too much to get to the top. Not only that, but you realize that you need to drop half of your values to continue. Cross out ten you can live without.

You know you need to get up to the peak. There is no going back. The only way to get off that island is by reaching the top. After a while, you know you have to lose more weight. Cross out another four values.

The climb continues. You are exhausted and close to giving up. The only way forward is to reduce your burden to three core values that no way could you live without. Cross out another three.

What are your three core values and what do they mean to you?

Core Value #1:

_____

_____

Meaning:

_____

_____

_____

_____

_____

_____

_____

_____

_____

_____

_____

_____

_____

_____

_____

Core Value #2:

_____

_____

Meaning:

_____

_____

_____

_____

_____

_____

_____

_____

_____

_____

_____

_____

_____

_____

_____

_____

_____

Core Value #3:

_____

_____

Meaning:

_____

_____

_____

_____

_____

_____

_____

_____

_____

_____

_____

_____

_____

_____

_____

_____

By defining your Why and values, you have defined the most significant aspects of your Marketing Engagement Language. This is something you should always share with everyone around you. You will always connect the most quickly and deeply with your audience with these two significant aspects at the forefront.

3

YOUR IDEAL CLIENT

"Choose your ideal clients so you work only with people who inspire and energize you."

—Michael Port

IT'S TIME TO FIGURE OUT who you need to work with to achieve your vision and live your story and values. You've figured out your Why(s) and your vision. Now it's time to figure out with whom you need to work! As soon as you start growing, which will happen soon after you identify your message, niche, and Marketing Engagement Language, the path will be more about what opportunities to avoid than waiting for opportunities to show up.

People who notice that you are consistent and congruent with the kind of person you truly want to serve will be attracted to you. The first time people reached out to me, I was so excited. All of a sudden, I had so many possibilities for spending my time.

I was approached by a large association and asked to launch a new franchise model for Mental Health Practices in Australia. This was a huge opportunity financially for me, but it didn't align with who I was and how I wanted to work. I turned it down because it was too far inside the western medicine approach and not close enough to alternative and holistic medicine for me.

After being a member of the Heal Yourself Expo committee in Queensland for three months, I stepped down to focus on my business. There was not enough time to work on that Expo every week due to my business, even though the Expo was a great chance to access my market.

You need to be clear about the core of your wellness business, which is your Why, your mission, and your ideal client. Otherwise, you'll have too much on your plate. Getting one thing right first will allow you to have time and money available which you can then use to your advantage. Dreams and ideals are all within our grasp, but to realize them, we have to take one step at a time.

ACTIVITY #5 - YOUR IDEAL CLIENT

Who is your ideal client?

It's not enough to know the demographics of your market. You need to know what drives your ideal client. Whenever I ask someone if they work with anyone or if they have a specific target audience, I often smile. The most common answer is something like, "I work with women between thirty-five and fifty-five who live in Australia and make over $100,000 a year." "That's great," I say, "but how does that help you with your marketing?" The response is mostly blank.

The idea that we should look at demographic information when it comes to our target market might be helpful for large advertising campaigns, since the agencies that use (and abuse) that information know how that affects their content and what they create. But this approach is almost useless for the average small business owner. You are not in the convincing or manipulating business. You are in the business of being yourself and attracting those who like you as you are.

In order to bridge the gap between the two, we need to understand the problems you solve, the results you generate, and the solutions you provide. Almost everyone goes online to find a solution to their problem that meets their needs. For example, my computer breaks down. My goal is to find the solution that suits me best by looking up phrases and words based on the outcomes I am looking for. In my case, when I first started my business, it was something like "refurbished MacBook pro". That's typical of what I Google. As you may know, I am a cash-short small business owner whose whole life is inside his computer and who loves Macs. If you sell refurbished Macs, I am your ideal customer. You can create content around why, how, and what can save me, your ideal client, money while still providing the best outcomes. Then, put your solution in front of me and tell me why I should buy from you.

In the service industry, the deeper you dive into the problems, outcomes, and solutions, the better connected you will be to your audience and the more interest you will generate.

To get started, think of the clients that you love working with the most – those you get the best results with and are willing to pay what you are worth. Think about your three best or favorite clients and what they expressed when you first talked to them. What did they say they wanted? What were they struggling with? Why did they want that and why did they struggle with that? By asking why, you can get to the heart of what motivates them. Knowing their problems will lead you to understanding their fears, and knowing their wants will lead you to understanding their dreams. Based on the work you did together, think about what those deeper issues and desires are. What would have happened if they hadn't resolved the issues they expressed to you? What would their lives have been like if they had gotten what they wanted?

You may have heard your clients say that they always feel stressed. What does that mean for their daily lives? Being unable to spend quality time with their family and friends? Are they always reactive, which impacts their productivity and relationships at work? When they say they want to live pain-free and get up in the morning with a spring in their step, what do they mean? Will they be able to do what they love? How can they become the best version of themselves?

In order to really connect with your audience, you need to under-stand the Why behind the first superficial answers. Choose three clients you loved working with, write their names in the table below, and explore their problems and fears, as well as their wants and dreams.

Favorite Client #1 Name:	**Favorite Client #2** Name:	**Favorite Client #3** Name:
Problems & Fears:	Problems & Fears:	Problems & Fears:
Wants & Dreams:	Wants & Dreams:	Wants & Dreams:

This is the time to put it all together and position yourself as the expert that you are. Your message, which incorporates all of your language, needs to be consistent and congruent across all channels. No matter where people come into contact with your business, be it your website, social media platforms, your networking pitch, and so forth, they should always come across the problems you solve, the outcomes you deliver, and the benefit-rich solutions you provide.

Let's bring it all together:

Problems:
Write down the three major problems from the table above:

_____

_____

_____

_____

_____

_____

_____

_____

_____

_____

_____

_____

_____

_____

_____

_____

Outcomes:

Write down the three major Outcomes from the table above:

_____

_____

_____

_____

_____

_____

_____

_____

_____

_____

_____

_____

_____

_____

_____

_____

_____

_____

_____

_____

_____

_____

_____

_____

_____

Solutions:

This can be a bit tricky but give it a go. Think about what you do so your clients work through a particular problem to achieve a certain outcome. Combine your solution with a "so that..." sentence to make your solution benefit-rich. Let me give you an example to make this clearer.

Let's say your problem is...

"You often react emotionally to others, not being able to respond from a place of deep connection to yourself which ultimately blocks you from finding your true purpose in life."

And the opposite to that (the outcome) is...

"Discover your emotional confidence to drop your protective behavior so you can open up your heart and tap into your soft and compassionate power."

A possible solution to that is...

"You need to find the wisdom in all your emotions and how they serve you, so that you can stay centered and strong in any situation."

You see how all three line up with each other and how strongly this comes across when you read this in one go? Try reading the above out loud using the following structure:

I help people who struggle with [problem] and would like to achieve [outcome]. I do this by showing them how to [solution]. How did this feel?

Write down the three major Solutions you provide to bridge the gap between the above problems and outcomes:

ACTIVITY #6 – YOUR ONE-LINER

The last step is to create a concise message in the form of the one-liner. Every tagline on your social profiles, your email signature, business cards, and so on should always be a similar statement. This is a one-liner, short, sharp, and punchy. Use the template below to create a first draft that you can perfect in the future.

I help _____ [insert ideal client group, e.g., business owners, Mums, people, etc.] who struggle with

_____

_____ *[insert main problem from the table]* to

_____

_____ *[insert main solution]* so they can

_____

_____ *[insert main outcome or two]*

> *Example: I help strong female leaders who think they have to constantly wear a protective mask, disconnecting them from others and themselves, to feel courageous again so they can find their compassionate power from their hearts and souls.*

Don't be too hard on yourself if you don't get this exercise right the first time. It's hard to do this on your own. The example above is from a client of mine; we created this by using my years of experience. Use this as a guide and a place to start. The only way to get it right is to start with a first version. It will change as you get feedback and grow. Starting off with a good foundation will put you miles ahead of the people around you.

Here are some tips to master sharing:

- Add a catchy hook: Insert something to your pitch that people will remember. Be creative – almost provocative. Evoke a reaction.
- Create emotions: Do not fear judgment from other people. If you say something with passion and enthusiasm, you will get both positive and negative reactions.
- Simplicity is key: Cut out all jargon and difficult terminology. Get to the point quickly!
- Improve all the time: Share whenever you can and if you don't get the right reaction, go back to the "drawing board". You will know when you get it right.

You are the prize – don't be desperate! If you talk to someone, adopt an attitude that says, "This will happen with or without you."

4

BECOMING A STORYTELLER

"Storytelling connects us with all of humanity."

—Kilroy J. Oldster, Dead Toad Scrolls

AS THE OLD SAYING GOES, "Facts tell, stories sell." The best way to really connect with your audience and express the value of your products is through stories. Those stories will create new stories within your ever-evolving business community. This is how great businesses that last a long time are created.

So, what are the stories that tell how you help others?

Write a story for each Problem, Outcome, and Solution above. Alternatively, you can combine one problem with one solution and outcome, but find at least three stories that you can use. Examine your past clients, friends, family members, celebrities, and your own life.

Show adversity, emotions, and feelings within your story rather than simply a timeline of facts. In the moment, it's not about finding the perfect story, but rather about laying the foundation for future marketing and exposure. When you write a blog article or social media post, or record a video telling one of these stories with clear examples of how your solution bridged the gap between the problems and outcomes you generated, people will get it and feel intrigued to know more. That is what the initial outreach through any of your channels is all about. Not to sell, but to create interest in more.

ACTIVITY #7 - YOUR STORIES

Your Story 1:

_____

_____

_____

_____

_____

_____

_____

_____

_____

_____

_____

_____

_____

_____

_____

_____

_____

_____

Your Story 2:

_____

_____

_____

_____

_____

_____

_____

_____

_____

_____

_____

_____

_____

_____

_____

_____

_____

_____

_____

_____

_____

_____

_____

_____

_____

_____

_____

_____

Your Story 3:

_____

_____

_____

_____

_____

_____

_____

_____

_____

_____

_____

_____

_____

_____

_____

_____

_____

_____

_____

_____

_____

_____

_____

These activities are a great way to find your niche and unique position, as well as what values you should run your business by and what vision and mission you have with your business. The foundation for creating meaningful connections with others rests on all of these factors. In some sense, everything you have read is focused on the same thing: the creation of deep and meaningful connections with other people. Creating these connections will make everything you do feel congruent and coming from the right place, and will make you feel happy and fulfilled in what you do.

In order to build a rock-solid foundation for all your future business endeavors, you must get it out there. Make sure you are consistent wherever you go. You should implement your new message, vision, mission, values, and stories in the following areas:

- Your website
- Social media profiles, posts and descriptions
- Industry business profiles and directories
- Email signature
- Pitch at networking events
- Any time someone asks you "What do you do?"

5

BEING TRUE TO YOURSELF

*"I'm unapologetic not because I'm strong-willed or
overconfident. I'm unapologetic because this is it; this is my life.
There is nothing I can do, no one I can please. I am a person
with a strong sense of being, that's all."*

—Jean Seberg

KNOW WHO YOU ARE and have the courage to stand by that in any situation. When I face change, disagreement with others, or even simply something new, I have to overcome basic fears and find courage to express my needs and opinions. It requires me to live unapologetically, but I want to do it with respect and humility because I want everyone around me to be able to do the same. If we disagree with something or someone, we can choose to communicate with respect. We can choose not to speak badly about others. We can choose to embrace change. We can choose to stand up for what we believe in and what we know is right for us. Expressing and being myself is a choice I can make unapologetically and with respect.

Having been in business for a long time, being unapologetic is one of the biggest lessons I learned, and it is a lesson I continue to learn all the time. In fact, it is not a lesson, but a process. There is always another facet of this I discover inside me.

In the small German village where I grew up, it was all about pleasing others and following the advice of others. This type of situation never allows you to be yourself. It makes you wear a mask. "But what would the people in the village think?" That was and still is (God bless her) my grandma's favorite saying. It's not surprising at all.

In her youth, the community was even stronger than it is today. People left their houses unlocked all the time. They walked in and out of each other's properties as needed and somehow respected each other's privacy as well. However, you had to learn so many unwritten rules, and most of them were all about managing what people around you would think of you.

My grandmother had a bad foot which made it almost impossible for her to walk. When I was a boy, her doctor told her the best thing for her would be to go for light walks so that the foot had a chance to straighten and keep up the movement it was supposed to do. The only flat surface was the street in front of her house, so we as her family suggested she walk around the church once a day for fifteen minutes. We never had a chance. It was impossible to get her to do that because of "what others would think". There was no clear purpose to this walk and what would others think if she just leisurely walked in the middle of the day on a working day. This fear was so strong that she is now in a wheelchair because she can't walk further than twenty meters.

It took us almost ten years to get her to use the wheelchair to go to the church across the street because she was afraid of how others would treat her. Once she conceded, to her surprise, people treated her with joy and love. Now that she knows everyone loves seeing her in the village and how lovely it is to be able to see and talk to her friends again, she loves it. Ten years of barely seeing her friends, all because of the stories she made up in her head!

It still drives me crazy. I love her with all my heart but this mindset is madness and not uncommon. People would prefer to sacrifice their health and lifestyle than risk the chance of stepping on each other's toes. It is truly infuriating, because the stories and fears behind this mindset are only a construct of the mind.

Our minds make up stories all the time. For example, I would create a new pitch for my business, but then I would fiddle around with it for ages before sharing it because I thought it wasn't quite right. Quite likely the pitch was not right, but how would I truly know if I didn't actually share it with a few people?

Whenever something new or a change comes up in life, our brain is wired to respond with the worst story possible and then hit "Repeat". This is based on evolution. When something changed in the campsite around the fire thousands of years ago, there could have been a predator. A change in the environment was a sign of life-threatening danger. So our brains learned to make us fear change and be incredibly resistant to it. In my opinion, this resistance to change has led many, including myself, to become stuck and unhappy because we can't truly express who we are and live the life we love most.

In order to live unapologetically, you must share and express your truth and what's right for you. That is probably one of the biggest obstacles to overcome. When we are in a good place and things are going well, it's all fun and games. When it is the opposite, we put on that mask. We give in to things that aren't quite aligned with us and can't say no. Don't compromise on the values you want to live by. Sometimes you have to push a little bit to keep on the path you have chosen and not get distracted, but it's important to keep the perspective on what's in front of you.

In the past, I hit obstacles with a lot of force. It was kind of in my nature. My beautiful partner Teresa always said, "It's like you are running against a wall over and over, head first, until the brick breaks. You finally broke through, but you did not notice that the wall was only two meters wide if you had stepped back a few meters."

These days, I'm all about going with the flow so I can keep perspective in life and see easier ways. However, the wall is not always only two meters wide and I might only need to push a little to keep moving forward. To know when to push through and when to back off and go around, you need to be in tune with your inner and outer selves.

I have learned how to look at matters more objectively, and I know I can rely on my intuition. The funny thing is that once you get the hang of balancing the Inner and Outer Games, bringing everything you do into alignment with who you truly are, you don't need to push or force anything.

Here's what I'll leave for you. To start, dig deeply and identify your Why(s). Once you have come to that realization, you will be able to comprehend the reality of the famous aphorism "know thyself". By understanding that you are coming from a place of love and care, and by defining your language that speaks to your audience, as we discussed, you can share your transformational values unapologetically. You can share your passion with the world so that everyone can see you for who you truly are. Thousands of people will be moved by this.And don't forget to have some fun along the way!

ABOUT THE AUTHOR

MY NAME IS SEBASTIAN HILBERT. I am a speaker, business consultant, and the co-founder of Wellnesspreneur.

I grew up in a small village in East Germany behind the Iron Curtain. Because of a lack of education and understanding of health, many people, including my friends and family, suffer from the Big 3: diabetes, cardiovascular disease, and cancer. It is heartbreaking for me to see the people I love and hold dearly suffer so much and the grief for those who have died is still with me. I can still feel my grandfather squeezing my hand on the night he died because the cancer took away his strength to speak.

After arriving in Australia in 2010, a whole new world of holistic health and wellbeing opened up to me and I decided to co-found Wellnesspreneur as part of fulfilling my vision ***to move the world to Sustainable Wellness.***

Since then, I have followed my heart and have helped dozens of wellness businesses grow to new heights and enabled them to make a bigger impact in this world.

ACKNOWLEDGMENTS

FIRST, I WANT TO THANK SONIA Armytage for the incredible editing work she has done. Her sincere care and understanding of what I genuinely want to share with the world has made this book a true representation of my work, passion, and expertise.

I thank my mother, Kathrin Hilbert, and father, Tino Hilbert, who set me up to live a bold life, full of love and joy. You have always encouraged me to believe in myself and do the things I love.

My life took a great turn when I met Ralph-Marc Diebold. Thank you from the bottom of my heart, my dear friend and mentor who saw greatness in me and sent me off to become a man on my own terms.

The depth and honesty of this book would only have been superficial at best without the support and encouragement from the love of my life, Teresa Armytage. I am forever grateful. My guide, my conscience, my muse.

Without the people close to me, this book could not have been a legacy that I could be proud of. Thank you, Stephen Armytage and Harry Armytage, for putting me on the right path for my writing.

Thanks to Wade Fransson and the whole publishing team at SOOP who saw the potential of this book and supported me in all aspects of my writing journey, from strategizing to marketing, editing and success coaching. You have been exceptional.

Thanks to my two co-editors Ben Jones and Tasso Dattenberg Doyle, who made a big impact in moving the book forward.

Last, but not least, thank you to my early sponsor Jeff Lougheed from Mealgarden who shared my vision *to move the world to Sustainable Wellness*.